Remembering Fort Myers

Remembering Fort Myers

The City of Palms

Prudy Taylor Board

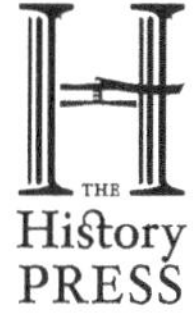

Published by The History Press
Charleston, SC 29403
www.historypress.net

Front Cover: Fort Myers, the City of Palms, derived its nickname from palm-lined McGregor Boulevard. *Courtesy of Southwest Florida Historical Museum.*
Back Cover: When Wild Bill Belvin returned from a year living off the land in North Fort Myers as a publicity stunt, Sheriff Frank Tippins, himself a colorful figure, arrested Wild Bill for stealing pelican eggs.

First published 2006

Manufactured in the United States

ISBN 978.1.59629.101.0

Library of Congress Cataloging-in-Publication Data

Board, Prudy Taylor, 1933-
Remembering Fort Myers : the city of palms / Prudy Taylor Board.
p. cm.
Includes bibliographical references.
ISBN 978-1-59629-101-0 (alk. paper)
1. Fort Myers (Fla.)--History--Anecdotes. 2. Fort Myers (Fla.)--Biography--Anecdotes. 3. Fort Myers (Fla.)--Buildings, structures, etc.--Anecdotes. I. Title.
F319.F74B63 2006
975.9'48--dc22
2006007408

Contents

Acknowledgements

My heartfelt thanks to Victor Zarick, Matt Johnson and the staff of the Fort Myers Historical Museum for sharing their time and research resources with me; their generosity was truly overwhelming. And a special thank you to Kathryn Wilbur for sharing so freely her time and personal photos and also to the Southwest Florida Historical Society, a group of splendid folks. And I must acknowledge my friend of many years, Maureen Bashaw, who always made room and time for me at "The Bashaw Inn" when I was in town doing research. Finally, words cannot express the gratitude I feel toward the News-Press and Lee Living and the other publications that have given me the opportunity to write about the hometown I love.

To my family—B.M. "Doc" Foster, my father; Louise Hingson, my mother; Don Hewitt, my uncle; Alma Hewitt Wells, my aunt; Melvie Hewitt Wonderly, my grandmother; and Herman L. Hingson, my stepfather—if they hadn't had the good sense to move to and stay in Fort Myers, I might have (shudder and gasp!) been born somewhere else. And to my daughter Jennifer Buckley and my son Byron Foster Taylor who put up with having a writer for a mother, seldom an easy task.

How Fort Myers Got its Name 1850

The man for whom Fort Myers was named was born in Georgetown, South Carolina, on May 14, 1811. Karl Grismer, writing in his book, *The Story of Fort Myers*, reports that Colonel Abraham C. Myers was the son of Abraham Myers, an attorney, and a descendant of Moses Cohen, the first rabbi in Charleston, South Carolina. Myers graduated from the U.S. Military Academy in 1833, was appointed a brevet second lieutenant and stationed at Baton Rouge, Louisiana.

Although he would distinguish himself many times during his career as an army officer, he would leave the service in disgrace. And just as his wife, Marion, was responsible for the naming of a fort (now a city) in her husband's honor, so would she inadvertently be responsible for his downfall.

Following the outbreak of the Second Seminole War, Myers was transferred to Florida and served there for two years. After Myers's first tour of duty in Florida, he served for a brief time in the West, and then was ordered back to Florida until the Second Seminole War officially ended when he was again transferred to the West. There he served under General Zachary Taylor in Texas and northern Mexico during the war between the United States and Mexico.

Myers was brevetted major for gallant and meritorious conduct in the battles of Palo Alto and Resaca de la Palma and then assigned to serve under General Winfield Scott. Myers took part in the battle of Churubusco, a small village six miles from Mexico City, which was considered one of the most important of the war. He was brevetted colonel for gallant conduct during that battle and served as chief quartermaster of the army of Mexico from April to June 1848.

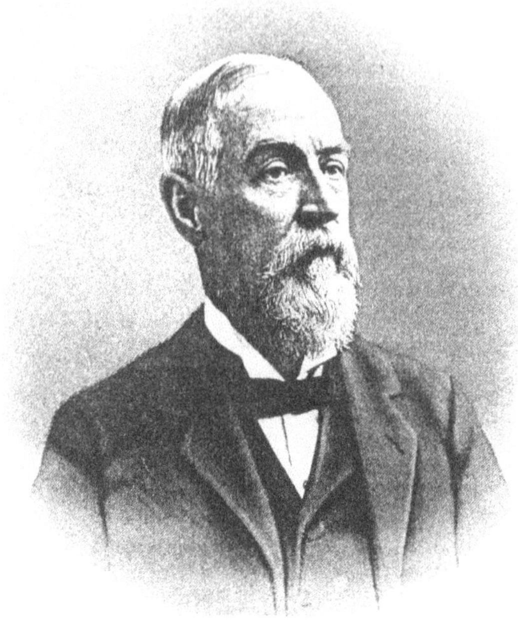

Colonel Abraham C. Myers, the man for whom Fort Myers was named. *Courtesy of Southwest Florida Historical Museum.*

In the years prior to the outbreak of the War between the States, Myers served at various Southern posts and at one time was chief quartermaster of the Department of Florida.

Local historian Walter Burke writes in his booklet *A Brief Account of the Life of Colonel Abraham Charles Myers, Quartermaster General, C.S.A.* that following the naming of Fort Myers in his honor in 1850, "Abraham C. Myers and Marion Twiggs [daughter of Major General David B. Twiggs] were soon married and from the union came four children, two daughters and two sons. One son, John Twiggs Myers (1871–1952), was a general in the U.S. Marine Corps and had a long and distinguished career."

In May of 1861, Warner continues, Twiggs was appointed major general in the provisional army of the Confederacy and assigned to command the District of Louisiana. Twiggs, seventy-one at the time, was the oldest officer of the United States Army to "take up arms for the Confederacy." Warner adds that Twiggs was soon compelled to retire because of his health and died on July 15, 1862, near Augusta, Georgia.

When the Civil War broke out, Myers was stationed in New Orleans, but resigned his commission and almost immediately joined the Confederate army. His father-in-law was now in command of the Department of Texas, according to *Generals in Gray: Lives of the Confederate Commanders*, by Ezra J. Warner. Warner writes, "His [Myers's] southern sympathies soon after induced him to surrender the military forces and stores under his command to Colonel [later General] Ben McCulloch, representing the State of Texas, an act for which he was dismissed from the United States service on March 1, 1861."

Myers, according to Grismer, was "appointed lieutenant colonel in the quartermaster general's department of the Confederate States Army on March 16, 1861. A few days later he was appointed acting quartermaster general and was raised to the rank of colonel on February 15, 1862." Burke adds that Myers was appointed permanent quartermaster general in December of 1861.

On March 20, 1863, the Confederate Congress passed a law providing "the rank, pay and allowances attached to the office of quartermaster general of the Army of the Confederate States shall be those of Brigadier General." According to Burke, this law was specifically passed to obtain for Myers the rank of brigadier general and to honor him. A letter endorsed by seventy-six members of the Confederate Congress recommending that Myers be appointed brigadier general was submitted to President Jefferson Davis shortly after that law passed.

However, President Davis had other ideas and responded with a letter published in Burke's biography of Myers which reads in part, "My own observation of Colonel Myers and the manner in which [he performs] the duties of quartermaster general satisfy me that the public interest requires an officer of greater ability and one better qualified to meet the pressing emergencies of the service during the war." The promotion was not forthcoming and on August 7, 1863, Myers was dismissed from the quartermaster's department when he refused to serve under his successor.

Both Grismer and Burke report that Myers faced many difficulties in carrying out his duties, which entailed providing all the supplies needed by the Confederate army. Grismer writes, "His bureau became the target of severe, unjustified criticism and on February 17, 1864, he was superseded by Brig. Gen. Alexander R. Lawton who had even less success in supplying the army's needs."

In addition, according to Burke, Davis harbored a strong dislike for Myers because it had come to his attention that Mrs. Myers had supposedly remarked that Mrs. Davis, who had a dark complexion, looked like a squaw. That interchange proved the end to Myers's military career. Grismer wrote, "Grieving over his dismissal from the quartermaster's office, he went to Georgia where he lived in retirement until the close of the war."

Burke's research uncovered a letter Myers later wrote on August 9, 1864, to General Braxton Bragg:

> *I made two visits to Augusta for the purpose of seeing you, feeling much my disappointment at failing to do so. My situation is painful in the extreme. Please let me know at an early day if the President means to drop my name from the Army list. Under laws creating a real army, I secured a place in it and should not be deprived of it, except by court martial. It is very humiliating to be obliged to live and depend very much upon the charity of friends, almost in want.*

At the end of the Civil War, Abraham C. Myers took his family to Weisbaden, Germany, where they lived for many years, returning to America in 1871. He died in Washington, D.C., on June 20, 1889.

Such irony—that Fort Myers would be born as the result of the storm which even today spawns fear and, as a military fort be named after a lover. Sad, too, that Myers would suffer both honor and dishonor at the hands of the woman he loved.

Originally published in "Only Yesterday" in the July 22, 1984 edition of the Fort Myers News-Press.

Lavish Expenditures
1856

Local taxpayers still reeling from cost overruns in connection with the East Lee County Sewer District and the Southwest Florida Regional Airport may take a measure of solace by noting that this area's first investigation into mismanagement and extravagance took place not in 1981, but in 1850. General David E. Twiggs, then in charge of federal troops in Florida, was instructed, as Karl Grismer writes, "to take all steps necessary for restraining the Indians."

Twiggs responded by reactivating and renaming Fort Myers. Grismer describes the activity that followed, writing, "Two more companies were sent to the Caloosahatchee, along with a force of carpenters, brick masons, and Negro laborers. This time there was nothing makeshift about the fort. The general's orders plainly stated that only the best materials were to be used."

Grismer considered what followed "a building boom, the first in the history of Southwest Florida," and wrote, "The first thing constructed was a substantial wharf built nearly 1,000 feet into the river a little west of what is now the foot of Hendry Street. At the end of the wharf there was a large platform, nearly 100 feet long, where boats docked. Supplies were taken to shore on a tram car for which rails were laid." And from there, the tracks led into a warehouse where supplies were stored.

Construction continued at a rapid pace until early 1856, when the War Department apparently became concerned about the amount of money being spent on construction at Fort Myers and called for an investigation. Upon orders from Major General T.S. Jessup, quartermaster general of the

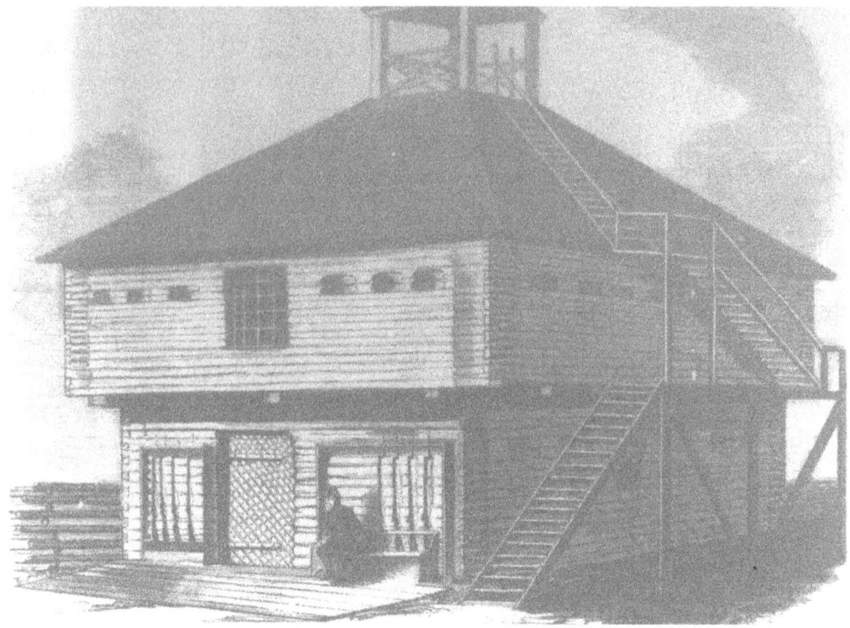

This sketch of a blockhouse at Fort Myers brought the fort its first exposure in national media when published in *Frank Leslie's Illustrated Weekly Guide* in the October 2, 1858 issue. It was done by Corporal C. Roller of Company G, Second Artillery. The building was not inside the blockade, but was located between present-day Hendry and Jackson Streets in the vicinity of Main Street. *Courtesy of Southwest Florida Historical Museum.*

U.S. Army, Assistant Quartermaster Major Justus McKinstry was sent to Fort Myers to investigate and report.

When McKinstry arrived, he found a military post composed of fifty-seven buildings. These included officers' quarters (with painted and plastered walls), enlisted men's barracks, a guardhouse, warehouses, sentry boxes, a blacksmith shop, a bake house, a laundry and quarters for the laundress, as well as a store. The store stocked tobacco, wines and whiskey for sale to the soldiers.

The buildings at the fort were frame and of yellow pine. The roofs of the permanent buildings were pine shingle, according to plans and specifications contained in McKinstry's report on file at the Fort Myers Historical Museum. The sidings were half-inch weatherboarding and, according to Grismer, the siding, floorings, doors, windows and shingles—which he maintains were cedar—were shipped in from Pensacola and Apalachicola.

In McKinstry's report, he merely notes that materials were "brought in vessels from a distance," not mentioning the ports. These buildings, incidentally, he estimated cost $5,110 to construct, adding that they cost less than projected.

The hospital, built just north of what is now the foot of Royal Palm Avenue, apparently occasioned special scrutiny; Grismer reports that its construction was begun in 1851 and that by the time it was completed several years later it had cost $30,000, according to Captain F.A. Hendry.

Reading the specifications today, it's obvious that the hospital was, by our standards, a modest three-story frame building. The heaviest parts of the frame were from timber "obtained in the vicinity of the post." Floors were tongue-and-groove dressed pine boards and the building was lathed and plastered throughout. Piazzas surrounded the first and second floors. These were of dressed pine boards and had plain railings.

On the first floor was the surgery with a planed, pine-board partition dividing it in half. Each side had a fireplace with a mantel. The second floor comprised three wards, two of which were connected with folding doors. Each ward also had a fireplace with mantels of dressed pine board.

The third floor had two wardrooms with chimneys passing through, but no fireplaces. Six dormer windows provided a view of the grounds. The hospital had been built by Assistant Quartermaster Captain A. Montgomery under the direction of Colonel Harvey Brown, then post commander.

Another item that drew McKinstry's attention was the bowling alley, for in his report he writes, "Same construction as sheds of stables with sides thatched with palmetto leaves. Pine board floor, planed. Understood to have been erected by the labor of soldiers not on extra duty and of materials not obtained from the Quartermaster's Dept."

In McKinstry's final report dated May 1856 and directed to General Jessup, he writes,

> *I have the honor to transmit plans and specifications of each and every structure at Fort Myers on the Caloosahatchee River, prepared under the direction of Capt. Hancock, A.Q.M. at that post, with a ground plan showing the relative position of the different buildings. With these data before you, no difficulty will be experienced in arriving at a conclusion as to how far your authority to erect the most temporary structures has been exceeded.*

McKinstry concludes, "I have no hesitation in stating that in my opinion buildings unnecessarily expensive have been erected, and that a lavish and uncalled for expenditure of the public money has been obtained at that post." Records are not available to determine what, if any, action resulted from the report.

On May 4, 1858, the fierce and fiercely intelligent Seminole Chief Billy Bowlegs and 124 of his people boarded the steamer *Grey Cloud*, which was docked at what is today the intersection of Hendry and Bay Streets, and departed for reservations in the West. This marked the conclusion of any action against the Indians and in June 1859, Fort Myers was once again deactivated and abandoned.

However, there's an interesting and ironic footnote concerning McKinstry's later career, which surfaces in historian Ezra Warner's book, *Generals in Blue: Lives of the Union Commanders*. In it, Warner describes Justus McKinstry as "chiefly celebrated for having been one of the most thorough going rogues ever to wear a United States uniform."

Warner reported that at the outbreak of the Civil War, McKinstry was in St. Louis as chief quartermaster of the Department of the West. While there, "he had found ample opportunity to line his own pockets at the expense of the government." Among gifts received from contractors who wished to do business with the U.S. Army in St Louis, Warner reported, was a $3,000 silver service for Mrs. McKinstry. He described the procedure by explaining that "one contractor would bill another for goods at an enormous advance in price; these goods would then be sold to the quartermaster's department at market."

According to Warner, one St. Louis contractor admitted making a profit of $280,000 on sales of $800,000 while McKinstry was in charge. Little wonder the contractors were grateful and generous.

> *Upon the succession of General David Hunter to command of that department, McKinstry's peculations* [embezzlements] *were investigated. And after a year in arrest, he was cashiered on January 28, 1863, "for neglect and violation of duty, to the prejudice of good order and military discipline," the only such sentence handed to a general officer to the War.*

It would be interesting to understand how a man so incensed about the construction of "buildings unnecessarily expensive" later became so blasé about "expenditures of the public money."

NOTE: Special thanks to local historians Stan Mulford and the late Walter E. Burke Jr. for their help in writing this series on the fort. Both men generously shared their research and Burke entrusted to me his library of books relating to Hancock and the generals.

Originally published in "Only Yesterday" in the September 2, 1984 issue of the Fort Myers News-Press.

Everyday Life at the Fort 1856

Fort Myers was six years old in February 1856 when Captain Winfield Scott Hancock was ordered to report for duty as garrison quartermaster. Hancock was one of the most famous and respected soldiers to serve at Fort Myers—he defeated General Robert E. Lee at the battle of Gettysburg and, although Hancock was stationed here for only fifteen months, he left his imprint on the area. Not only was he so highly respected as a soldier, but also his daughter, Ada, was the first child born in Fort Myers. Furthermore, local historians are indebted to his wife, Almira, who described life at the fort in a book titled *Reminiscences of Winfield Scott Hancock*, which was published in 1887, the year following Captain Hancock's death. In that book, Mrs. Hancock wrote of being the only woman on the post.

> *To many this might have been a deplorable experience, cut off as we were from civilization and suffering all the inconveniences of a frontier station. Our mail came from Tampa Bay in a sailboat, and wind and wave permitting, was received once a week. Commissary stores and other supplies came in the same way, and on one occasion, when the boat capsized with a load of these stores, we were without some of the necessities of life for six weeks.*

Traveling with the Hancocks was their son, Russell, and the need for milk was a problem.

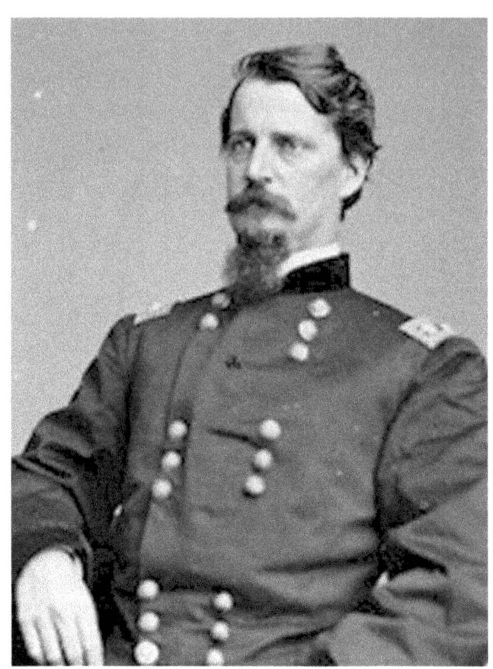

General Winfield Scott Hancock. *Photo from author's archives.*

> *Gail Borden* [the inventor of condensed milk and founder of the Borden Company] *was unknown then, and milk could only be obtained from the half-starved, Florida cows. Fort Myers could not boast such an animal as a milk cow and Mr. Hancock made four separate attempts before we could secure such a luxury…*
>
> *The first cow strayed from the herd during the overland journey, and never reached us; the second came by sea and while being landed at the dock fell overboard and broke her neck; the third was safely landed but wandered into a quicksand on the day of her arrival and so was lost. Persistency was finally rewarded and the fourth attempt was successful.*

Life at Fort Myers during the 1850s was complicated not only by the presumed constant threat of Indian attack and the basic rigors of military life, but by the weather as well. Soldiers were massing to fight Billy Bowlegs in the Everglades, and for that reason the quarters within the stockade were full. As a result, a number of soldiers and officers were camped about a mile from the fort. Mrs. Hancock wrote of the conditions in camp during this cramped and crowded time.

> *During rainy season the storms were frequently so severe and so prolonged that no fires could be lighted or cooking done in camp. Pork for the men was cooked in the fort, while the officers fared as best they could. During this time, I kept open house, and the table was always stretched to full capacity. The officers drew lots for this privilege and chance decided who should be our guests at breakfast, luncheon and dinner.*

She reported, too, that freedom of movement was very restricted because the Seminoles were so close. In fact, her walks were limited to the long wharf that extended into the Caloosahatchee River. "The river offered another diversion, and we often embarked on the current of the stream in a well-manned barge, and with the oarsmen well armed," she wrote.

On several occasions, she wrote that Indians were discovered on the banks of the river. When this happened, she and her son, Russell, stretched out on the bottom of the boat and were covered with a heavy rubber blanket. Mrs. Hancock writes with humor of one such time when it was discovered "that the stalwart Indians in their flaming red blankets were nothing but poor flamingoes, innocent of any evil intent, and occupied with efforts to secure a dinner." Mrs. Hancock writes of the encroachments of the Indians upon the camp itself.

> *The monotony of garrison life was occasionally relieved by the startling sound of the long roll beaten at night, as a signal of attack (or supposed attack) from the Indians. Preparations were immediately begun for a transfer to the blockhouse, and this was to be accomplished in the dark, as the orders prohibiting light in quarters were imperative.*

In each instance during her tenure here, the alarms were false, occasioned by some intoxicated soldier's effort to pass the guard in Indian style, on hands and knees, under the sentry boxes that were suspended ten, twelve, or more feet above ground. However, so great was the tension at the fort that every such attempt resulted in the soldier's death.

> *One of the sentries, a most worthy man, killed his best friend in this way, which so preyed upon his mind as to unfit him ever afterwards for service and his discharge was recommended. He would desert his post when on guard, asserting that his dead friend appeared to him reproachfully, and he could not understand why others could not see what to him was so real.*

The Hancocks' son, Russell, then four, was to play a role in a seemingly unimportant but revealing incident. Describing it as "a little episode worth repeating," Mrs. Hancock writes of a council of war called by General William S. Harney, then commander of the federal troops in Florida. During that council, Harney ordered that captured Seminole women and their children be brought to appear before him so that he might secure information concerning the location of Billy Bowlegs's camp in the Everglades.

> *Our little son Russell was sitting with his father listening with baited breath to General Harney's threat, given through an interpreter, of hanging the papooses who were playing at the feet of their mothers unconscious of any danger. Unable any longer to endure the suspense, especially when the General brought forth a formidable looking rope, which Russell thought was being used in a very reckless way, he sprang from his seat and commenced pleading piteously for the lives of the little Indian babies. Finding the General inexorable, he finally gave it up, and in deepest grief exclaimed, "Well, if you will hang them, please give me their bows and arrows." The General remarked afterward, "That boy spoilt all our fun and we had to give it up until another time."*

Mrs. Hancock reported that General Harney revealed that his attempts to extort information from the Seminole women were futile.

In concluding her comments concerning their tour of duty at Fort Myers, Mrs. Hancock describes the area as "this forsaken country, prodigal only in the number and variety of venomous snakes and insects of every kind," adding, "however, that here our sweet child Ada was born—sole daughter of our house and home."

Ada Hancock, the first child born in Fort Myers, was to die young. In *Hancock the Superb* by Glenn Tucker, the author describes Ada as

> *Hancock's greatest joy. He had her portrait painted by a celebrated artist of the time, B.F. Reinhart. It shows a soft, sensitive-looking girl with clear, clean features, large blue eyes, high forehead and tresses that must have reached her waist. She read much and the general lavished books on her; some of the best literature of the day was in her library. Then when she was 19, she contracted typhoid fever. She died after a brief illness on March 28, 1875. No other loss had ever struck the general such a blow.*

However, there were to be other great losses; Hancock's grandson and namesake died in 1880 and his son Russell died in 1884.

A graduate of the 1844 class at West Point, Hancock—for whom Hancock Bridge Parkway in North Fort Myers was named—went on to distinguish himself in a number of battles during the Civil War, including those at Spotsylvania and Gettysburg.

Perhaps the highlight of his career occurred in June 1880 at the Democratic National Convention in Cincinnati when he was nominated to be the Democratic candidate for president of the United States. He was defeated that November by James A. Garfield, but the race was close. According to the *Encyclopedia of American Facts and Dates* the electoral vote was 214 to 153, but the popular vote found Garfield to be the victor by fewer than 7,000 votes.

Hancock died on February 9, 1886, at Governor's Island in New York Harbor. He and his daughter are buried in Montgomery Cemetery in Norristown, Pennsylvania, his birthplace.

Originally published in "Only Yesterday" in the August 19, 1984 edition of the Fort Myers News-Press.

The Battle of Fort Myers 1865

Historians disagree on the details. Some label it a skirmish, while others call it a bloody battle. Whatever the nomenclature, all agree that it was the southernmost engagement of the War between the States, and that it took place in Fort Myers on February 21, 1865.

Fort Myers was abandoned in 1858 following the Seminole Wars and was deserted until the Civil War, except for a brief period when it was occupied by a civil force that was studying tropical plants, according to Captain F.A. Hendry in *A History of the Early Days in Fort Myers*. According to Hendry, the war caused the botanical project to be abandoned.

Although Fort Myers was quite a distance from the major action of the war, the area did play a prominent role as a supplier of cattle. Karl Grismer wrote,

> *By the time the Civil War began, Florida was one of the leading cattle states in the South. With the beginning of the hostilities, the Confederate Army started making heavy inroads on Florida herds. Meat provided by the scrub cattle may have been stringy and tough but it was better than no meat at all. Besides, the cattle were urgently needed for their hides and tallow.*

In his book, *Florida During The Civil War*, Dr. John E. Johns said the times were difficult and Florida was filled with deserters. "They preferred to 'lay out,'" he wrote, "that is, to secret themselves near their homes, if possible. The controlling motive...was not love for the Union. They were actuated almost entirely by the desire to remain out of Confederate service."

Johns explained that serving with the Confederacy would have led to the immediate confiscation of their land and homes by the Union. Additionally, he wrote, many men deserted because of concern for their families. Financially, the state was heavily burdened and could not provide for the needy families.

Johns wrote that the situation "became so critical in Taylor County that a petition was sent to Jefferson Davis, signed by the county officials, asking that all males between the ages of 18 and 45 be exempt from conscription." Officials said that if more men were taken from the area, "widespread starvation would occur among the women and children."

Authors A.J. and Kathryn Hanna, in their book, *Lake Okeechobee: Wellspring of the Everglades*, said that General David P. Woodbury, Federal commander at Key West, received word that there were between two hundred and eight hundred Union sympathizers lurking "in the woods between Lake Okeechobee and Charlotte Harbor," and that these men would join the United States if a post were established in the area. The Hannas wrote that Woodbury proposed to send the Florida Rangers—nineteen Union sympathizers who had formed a company in Key West—and a company of regulars to "some spot" in Charlotte Harbor and the group left Key West on December 17, 1863, arriving six days later.

"Apparently," the Hannas wrote, "there was no opposition to the Federal approach from the settlers nor from the meager Confederate forces to the north. By January 7, 1864, the Federals moved to Fort Myers." The Union leaders intended, first, to cut off the supply of cattle to the Confederates, and second, to use the fort as a haven for refugees and a center for raiding parties.

Grismer wrote, "Five companies of regular Federal troops and the small company of Florida Rangers moved into the fort late in December 1863, and all the munitions and provisions needed were brought in from Key West. The buildings were found to be in excellent condition, despite the fact that they had been abandoned 4½ years." One of their first actions, according to Grismer, was to build a breastwork of earth and logs near what is now the Edison Bridge.

The Union raids against the cattle supply did prove effective. As Hendry wrote later, "The Federal soldiers took possession of Fort Myers and made it headquarters for all the men much to the distress of devotees of the Southern cause. Large herds of cattle were rounded up by Federal Cavalry and driven to Fort Myers and there slaughtered for use by the garrison and blockading squadrons of Sanibel Island in San Carlos bay, and a large number carried on transport to Pine Island, landing about where St. James is now situated." Grismer wrote that between January 1, 1864, and the end of the war, at least forty-five hundred head of cattle were taken by the Federals.

And the situation was serious enough that the Confederates organized the Cattle Guard Battalion, or the "Cow Cavalry," which was really a home-guard outfit. Grismer said it was composed of settlers exempted from service "because they owned 500 head of cattle or more, and were needed at home to guard their property."

Hendry described the battle of February 21, writing,

> *A day was spent in cannon and rifle practice, one of those bloodless battles. One man was killed. A lot of pickets, horses and cattle captured was* [sic] *the result so far as Major Footman, but the most desired result was going on in the front. While Footman was retracing steps having given up the undertaking as a bad job, the Federals were packing up and hurrying down the river to Punta Rassa.*

Grismer labeled this account as a "tale [that] has all the earmarks of being embellished by imagination." His version is very different. According to Grismer, the motivation for the battle was accurate. Colonel Munnerlyn became so irked by the raids out of Fort Myers that he decided the fort must be destroyed.

"To accomplish this feat," Grismer writes, "he sent out a force of 275 men, armed with one field piece, under the command of Major William Footman. The major approached the fort on Feb. 21 and formally demanded the surrender within 20 minutes. His demand ignored, the major opened fire with one piece of artillery. All day long the 'attack' continued with the Federals answering with their three field pieces." By dark, when Major Footman determined the fort could not be taken, he withdrew after capturing a few horses and pickets.

The Hannas gave short shrift to the battle of Fort Myers, writing merely,

> *In February 1865, Major Footman attempted an attack on the Federals at Fort Myers with 400 soldiers and one piece of artillery. Before opening fire, he sent a demand to the fort, which was garrisoned by refugees and Negro forces, to surrender within twenty minutes. The fighting, which*

followed refusal of this demand, lasted about one-half day on February 21. Before night fell the Confederates withdrew. Nothing was won beyond the capture of a few horses.

The exact truth may well lie buried and moldering in military records stored in the National Archives. Historians do agree, however, that there was a battle of Fort Myers and that it was the southernmost confrontation of the War between the States.

Originally published in "Only Yesterday" in the April 12, 1985 edition of the Fort Myers News-Press.

The Gardner-Kelley Home

1884–1992

Paint peeling, windows broken, the 108-year-old Gardner-Kelley Home is a sad wraith, a ghost of its former beauty. Never a showplace in the style of the Edison, Ford and Burroughs winter homes, it was nonetheless architecturally and historically important because it was a year-round home to two families prominent in Lee County's history. And it has witnessed many changes throughout its existence. At the time it was constructed during the winter of 1884–85, the village of Fort Myers numbered approximately 350 hardy souls; a far cry from the 44,000 that call it home today. Our streets bustled with cowboys, businessmen in high-starched collars, ladies carrying parasols and wearing button shoes and Seminoles in vivid, multi-hued jackets.

The grounds of the Gardner-Kelley Home were important to the Seminoles for that's where they used to gather. They camped beneath the sheltering branches of the now 175-year-old twin oaks on the grounds. And Gardner's property, a twenty-four-acre tract that took up the entire block, was one of the largest holdings in the village. It was bounded by Second and Lee Streets and Anderson (now Dr. Martin Luther King Jr. Boulevard) and Royal Palm Avenues. Reverend Gardner purchased the land from Captain F. A. and Ardeline Hendry for the sum of $3,500.

William Philbrick Gardner, a minister in the Methodist Episcopal Church, came to Fort Myers from Louisiana during the winter of 1884–85 with his wife, his son Albertus A. (Bertie) and his daughter, Miranda Melvina (Miss Minnie). The family was forced to move to a milder climate because of Mrs. Gardner's health.

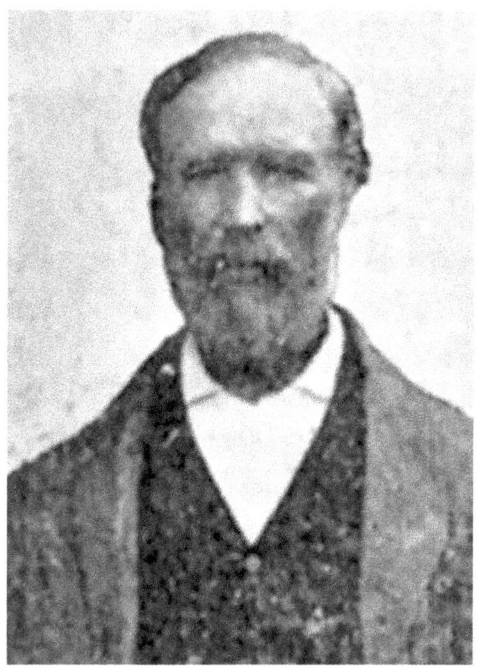

Reverend William Philbrick Gardner arrived in Fort Myers in 1884 and that same winter built the home that would become known as the Gardner-Kelley House. *Courtesy of Southwest Florida Historical Society.*

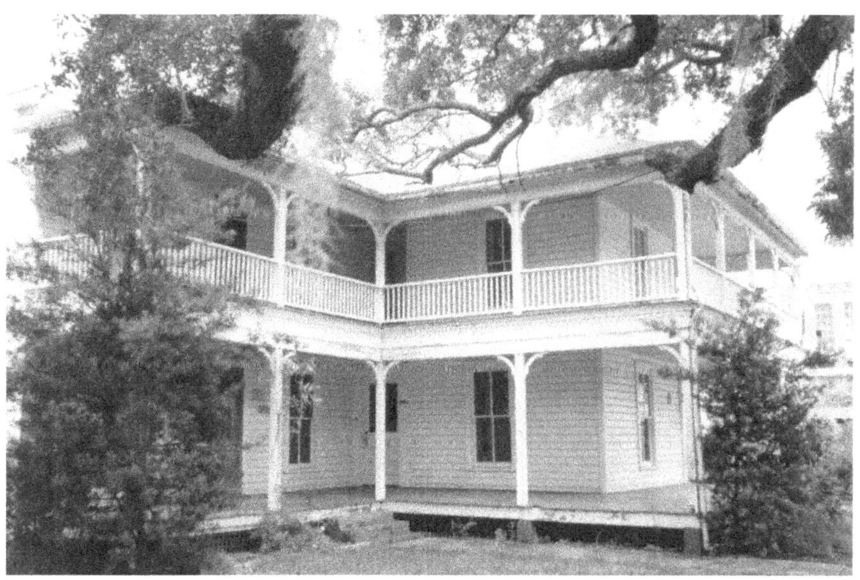

The Gardner-Kelley house, built in 1884–85, with its wraparound porch was an excellent example of a home built for year-round living in Fort Myers. This photo was taken in 1990 shortly before its demolition. *Courtesy of Southwest Florida Historical Society.*

They chose an exciting time to arrive. Thomas Alva Edison had visited for the first time earlier that year and bought land for his home. The *Fort Myers Press* had published its first issue in November. In fact, Reverend Gardner had been one of the local businessmen who encouraged Stafford C. Cleveland, "kidnapped" owner and editor, to establish his newspaper in Fort Myers. Cleveland's original destination was Fort Ogden, but when the captain of the steamboat on which Cleveland was traveling learned Cleveland was a newspaper editor and had a press in cargo, the captain sailed past Fort Ogden and docked at Fort Myers instead. Gardner even pledged $600 to help Cleveland defray his start-up expenses.

In 1885, the villagers voted to incorporate Fort Myers as a town largely so they would have local law enforcement and government. Since Fort Myers was part of Monroe County, the county seat and the sheriff's office had been located in Key West.

Built during the winter of 1884–85, the Gardner-Kelley House is of frame vernacular design. Its highlights include a two-story verandah, the original pressed metal roof and an ornamental fence with poured concrete benches. The small garage on the grounds was built between 1909 and 1914 for Miss Minnie's electric car.

The Gardner family entered enthusiastically into the activities of the fledgling city, an involvement that continued for more than fifty years. In 1887 during an outbreak of the dreaded yellow fever, it was Gardner as acting mayor who soothed and reassured the frightened villagers, according to the *Press*.

> *Yellow Jack is a disease that feeds on and revels in filth. And since our town is noted for cleanliness and perfect drainage, the scourge cannot find a lodgment here. Our quarantine regulations are strict and are being rigidly enforced and we think we have no reason to fear. Keep a brave heart, live frugally, and guard your person and premises, and all will be well.*

In addition to being active in local government, Reverend Gardner continued to function as a minister, but moved into the business sector as well. In 1888, he and his family founded the Seminole Canning Company. A report published in the *Jacksonville Times Union* revealed that:

> *Fort Myers has the distinction of producing more than half the guava jelly made in the United States. It is manufactured by the Seminole*

> *Canning Company...Their jellies are known and appreciated all over the country and are noted for their purity and excellence. The factory has a capacity of 7,000 pounds a week, and, in addition to their guava, they make also a very superior quality of orange and lemon jelly. All their boxes, cans and other material are made on the premises. Their guava grove is perhaps the best remaining in the state. The place passed uninjured through the freeze and their oranges, lemons, limes, grapefruit, persimmons, bananas, etc. are in fine condition.*

In addition to the fruits they grew, the Gardners contributed to the local economy by buying guavas from local people and paying them twenty-five to forty cents a bushel. The Gardners also hired as many as fifty workers to make the jellies and preserves and were one of the largest employers in the area.

Gardner served Fort Myers and Lee County in many other capacities. In 1886, he was one of the organizers of the Fort Myers Cemetery Company along with F.A. Hendry, W.M. Hendry, T.E. Langford, and J.J. Blount. From Major James Evans, the men purchased a forty-acre tract of land on what is now Michigan Avenue and townspeople paid the sum of fifty dollars to bury their loved ones within its confines. Today the City of Fort Myers owns and operates that cemetery, and the rates are still reasonable.

By the time he died in 1898, Gardner had been supervisor of elections, chairman of the Board of Public Instruction and president of the Board of Health in addition to being a member of the Town Council and acting mayor.

The importance of the Gardner family to Fort Myers and Lee County cannot be overstated. Long after their father died, Bertie and Minnie carried on his legacy of service to the community. Operating always as partners, they continued to run the canning company, but by that time, brother and sister were in still another business: the business of supplying electricity.

On October 9, 1897, the town council granted Bertie Gardner a five-year franchise and agreed to pay him $300 annually for ten streetlights. By the end of the year, he had installed a forty-horsepower boiler and a five-hundred-light dynamo (generator) in the canning plant. The evening of January 1, 1898, the streets of Fort Myers were illuminated for the first time and, for the first time, townspeople could walk the streets after dark without carrying lanterns.

Two and a half years later, Bertie Gardner and Miss Minnie were responsible for providing still another modern convenience to Fort Myers residents. They invested $5,500 in ice-making equipment, which Bertie also installed in the canning factory. On May 22, 1901, the first ice was sold at the factory for 50¢ for one hundred pounds. Delivered, the price was a penny a pound. Bertie Gardner told the *Press* he had $18,000 invested in the three operations, which were then officially known as the Seminole Power & Ice Company.

In 1913, Gardner sold the Seminole Power & Ice Company to Engineering & Utilities of New York for $104,000. Later the company name was changed to Southern Utilities. Southern Utilities sold the power and ice plants to Florida Power & Light in 1925.

The home was sold to Mr. and Mrs. James B. Kelley in 1947. That portion of the property that had been used as the canning plant was detached, moved to face Second Street and sold to Lynn Gerald, a young lawyer who later became a prominent Lee County circuit court judge. The Kelleys lived in the home nearly forty years. Mr. Kelley was also very active in the community. In addition to serving on a number of civic committees, he was elected to the Fort Myers City Council and was one of Lee County's most successful realtors. In 1987, Mr. Kelley, then a widower, sold the home to the First Presbyterian Church, which intended to use the land for a parking lot.

In 1991, the ice plant was leveled and Fort Myers lost a gigantic slice of its history. Stringent efforts are now being made by the Southwest Florida Historical Society to see to it that the Gardner-Kelley Home is not lost as well.

At this writing, Mayor Wilbur Smith has indicated he will approach the City Council to purchase the home with the goal of restoring it to the era of the 1880s and opening it to the public as an addition to the historical homes tour. The Historical Society has agreed to raise monies for the restoration once the home has been acquired by the City. Because the architecture is so different from the Edison, Ford and Burroughs homes, the Gardner-Kelley Home is of inestimable value as a resource to demonstrate everyday life in Fort Myers in the 1880s, arguably the most dynamic decade in Lee County's history, leading up to the county's founding in 1887.

UPDATE: The efforts of citizens failed and in 1992, the Gardner-Kelley House was leveled. Ironically, the house was leveled late Friday afternoon as the Florida Historical Society was holding its annual convention in Fort Myers. The area is now used as a parking lot by the First Presbyterian Church.

Originally published in the April 1992 issue of Lee Living.

The Murphy-Burroughs Home

1901

The Murphy-Burroughs Home at the intersection of First and Fowler Streets in downtown Fort Myers was a showplace for many years. Its twin chimneys and widow's walk are remnants from a time when the paving of First Street was not yet even an idea and when a sidewalk meandered along the banks of the Caloosahatchee in front of the home.

The construction of the home was a grand event and trumpeted on the front page of the *Fort Myers Press* in October of 1899 with headlines that declared it to be "A Palatial Residence."

John T. Murphy, the man responsible for the home's construction, was described in the *Press* as being "from Helena, Montana, a wealthy mine owner and stock man who was delighted with his stay here last winter and became interested in orange groves."

Murphy and his friend D.A.G. Floweree had been visiting in Tampa and had read a story in the *Tampa Tribune* that Florida was having "the biggest trade in its history and that thousands of steers were being shipped out of Punta Rassa to Cuba." The same article referred to Fort Myers as the cow capital of the state so Murphy and Floweree decided to have a look. They apparently weren't impressed with Florida's lean, stringy range cattle, but instead were charmed by Fort Myers's tropical beauty.

Murphy selected local businessman H.E. Heitman to act as his agent and purchased 450 feet of riverfront property for $3,500. Later, he sold about half of that to Floweree. Murphy and Floweree had wanted that same parcel, but Murphy won a coin toss and his home was built on the corner

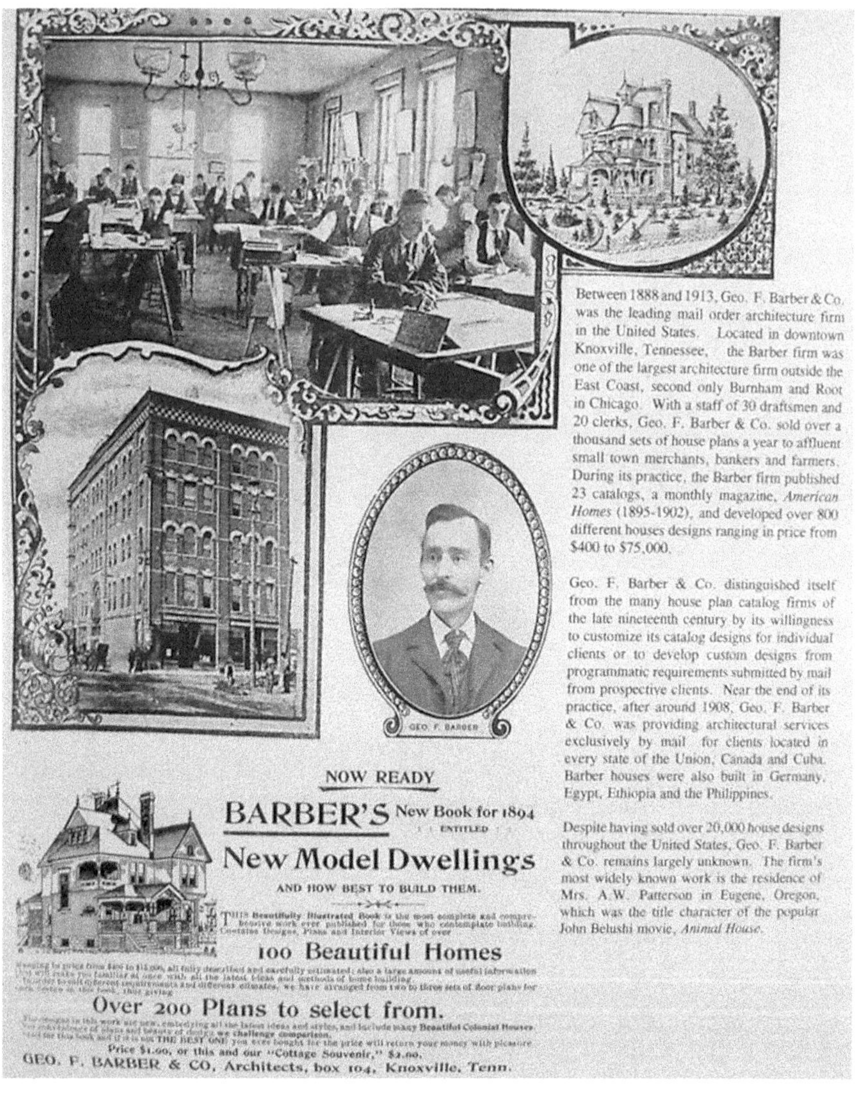

George F. Barber. *Photo from author's archives.*

lot. His friend, also a prosperous cattleman from Iowa, bought the adjacent land. Floweree built a home next to Murphy's, but his home was torn down in the late 1950s and an apartment building was erected on the site.

The *Fort Myers Press* dutifully recorded each stage of construction. One reporter expressed his enthusiasm by writing, "We have looked over the plans and specifications and should say that this new residence is to be one of the handsomest south of Tampa."

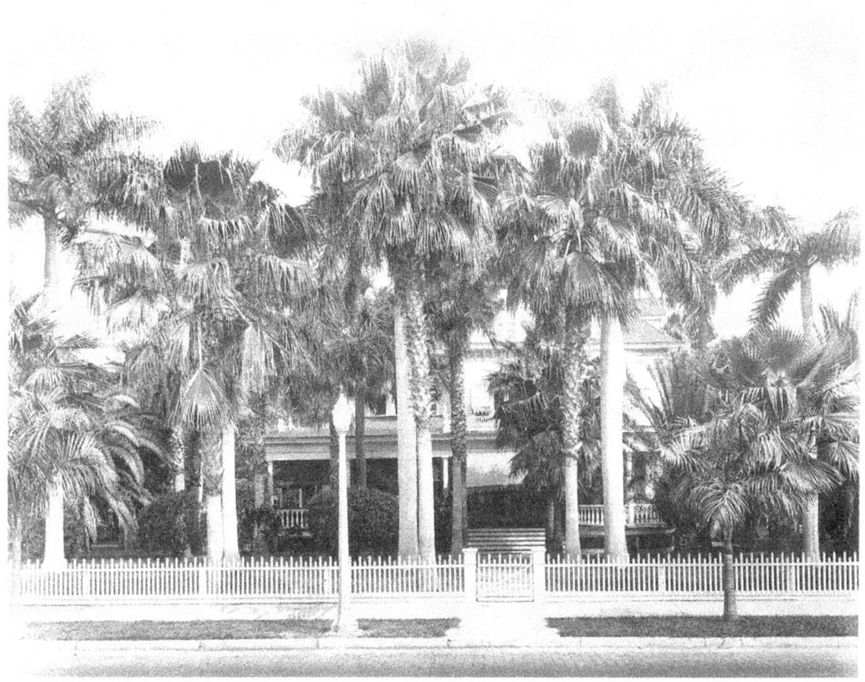

The Murphy-Burroughs Home in 1901. *Courtesy of Southwest Florida Historical Museum.*

Local contractors were invited to bid, but the paper announced that contractors from Punta Gorda, Tampa and Jacksonville were also submitting bids. C.S. Caldwell of Tampa was the successful bidder. The architect was G.F. Barber of Knoxville, Tennessee.

Barber, very prominent in architectural circles, mass-marketed his designs by printing and selling pattern books. Furthermore, Barber was not only an architect; he was well versed in carpentry and drafting as well as being an extremely astute businessman. In addition to plans, he provided building materials and eventually complete house kits—actually prefabricated homes. The crated materials arrived by boxcar.

The Murphy–Burroughs Home, however, was designed by Barber exclusively for the Murphy family and was not built from a kit. As described in Barber's plans, there was to be an eleven- by sixteen-foot reception hall, a fifteen- by sixteen- foot parlor facing onto First Street, a fifteen- by sixteen-foot sitting room overlooking Fowler Street, a fifteen- by-seventeen foot library and a dining room measuring thirteen and a half feet by seventeen feet. All of these rooms were on the first floor and were finished in curly pine and with heart of maple floors. The rooms were extremely large for Fort Myers homes during that period.

In addition to the spacious verandahs encircling the house on the first floor, there would be balconies on the second floor opening from the five sleeping rooms, which also included a sitting room in the center and two bathrooms. The third floor was composed of four large rooms that were later used as servants' quarters.

The house was truly modern for its time since it was lighted by electricity, had electric bells throughout and an annunciator (an early version of an intercom) in the kitchen to summon the servants.

Construction started in March of 1900 and Murphy occupied the home in 1901. The home cost $15,000 to build, an absolutely staggering sum for the day. In addition to the investment Murphy had made in the home, the importance of its construction in the small town was that it focused attention on Fort Myers as a winter home for the wealthy and socially prominent. It also set a standard for the construction of other similar homes. Although Edison had built his winter home here, he had not visited for a number of years and Fort Myers had languished. In fact, Floweree rented from Edison while waiting for his home to be completed.

Even when Edison stayed in Fort Myers, he was not one to host brilliant social galas. His friends, while industrial magnates, were not socialites. As a result of Murphy's arrival, Fort Myers's social scene changed and the young town began to attract a different type of winter visitor.

Murphy and Floweree had still further impact on the community. When they first arrived, the riverfront was dirty and strewn with litter. The wharves and docks were old and rundown. Murphy and Floweree cleaned up the riverbank in front of their homes and constructed a private seawall, again setting an example the city soon followed.

Murphy wintered here for many years and became active in local business circles. He was one of the organizers of the Lee County Bank, which acquired a national charter and changed its name to the First National Bank in January of 1908. (The First National Bank building still remains on First Street directly across from the Bradford Hotel.)

During the Spring of 1914, while vacationing in Fort Myers, Murphy contracted pneumonia. Returning to Montana, he died May 22, 1914, at his home in Helena, leaving the Fort Myers home to his wife, Clara Cobb Murphy. After Murphy's death, she never returned but sold the property to Walter G. Langford, president of the First National Bank. Langford made a number of improvements to the house while he and his wife and two daughters, Faye and Buena, lived there. He added a tennis court, a garage, a gazebo and a sixty-foot water tower.

In 1918, Langford sold the home to Howard Cole, a wealthy investment broker and bachelor from New York. Cole was engaged to a young woman who did not want to live in Fort Myers. As result, in August of 1919, he sold the home to Nelson Thomas Burroughs of Chicago, Illinois.

Burroughs was also an extremely successful businessman with interests in banking, cattle, land and lumber. Burroughs and his wife, Adeline, had four children: two sons, Roy and Raynor, who died young and two daughters, Mona and Jettie.

In May of 1922, Burroughs transferred the title to the house to Mona and Jettie and continued wintering there until his death in 1932. The daughters moved into the home and lived there year-round. Jettie remained unmarried, but Mona was married three times.

Mona's first husband, Joseph Wandrack, an all-American football player in college, was reportedly the love of her life. However, he died around age fifty-nine from what was described as an "athlete's heart condition." John McCurdy was her second husband. Her third husband was Franz Fischer. She was widowed twice.

After Mona's death in 1978, the home was given to the City of Fort Myers by her copersonal representatives. Fischer, her third and surviving spouse, retained the right to the use and occupancy of the property for the remainder of his lifetime. He died in 1983.

The Burroughs Home was the center for many of Fort Myers's social activities in the early years. The Thomas Edisons and the Henry Fords were the regular guests. An undated clipping from the *Press* reports,

> *The beautiful Burroughs Home on First Street was the scene of one of the most brilliant and charming entertainments of the winter season. Following a reception in the spacious front rooms, the 150 guests were served with delicious punch on the rear verandah and then went to the moonlit tropical gardens. A grand march, a Virginia Reel and dancing were enjoyed upon the concrete tennis court. Peter van Deuyl's orchestra furnished the music for the dancing. Two banjo and guitar artists also entertained the guests with music and song.*

After Fischer's death, the City of Fort Myers took possession of the house and property. Mayor Oscar Corbin appointed a Board of Trustees that was successful in placing the property on the National Register of Historic

Places. A preservation and management plan, funded in part by a grant from the Historic Preservation Fund, was used as a guide for the restoration plans. It was opened to the public and placed on Fort Myers's Historic Homes Tour in April 1990.

Today the Murphy-Burroughs Home has been restored and although the city of Fort Myers has changed dramatically in the intervening years, the Murphy-Burroughs Home remains a showplace. Yet even today its lovely tropical grounds echo with bright conversation and laughter for, in addition to the public tour, the home is booked year round with private parties and weddings.

Immokalee, the name given to the home by Murphy, is a Seminole word meaning "my home." Located on a 2.45-acre site on the Caloosahatchee River, the home is of Georgian Revival architecture. The 2 ½-story structure has a symmetrical facade, Palladian windows, bay windows and a deep verandah supported by wooden columns and pilasters that gird three sides of the house. The east porch was destroyed by Hurricane Donna in September of 1960 and rebuilt.

The house is sided with cypress clapboard painted yellow. The steep hip roof is constructed of asphalt shingles over the original cypress shakes and has a deep, dentiled eave. The roof terminates with a balustraded widow's walk between paired brick chimneys. Each side of the roof has two gabled dormers.

The Men of the Murphy-Burroughs Home

Born February 26, 1842, in Platte County, Missouri, Murphy was only seventeen when he left his paternal home and traveled to Colorado where he worked as a clerk. By 1864, he had saved enough money to outfit a wagon train with merchandise geared to meet the needs of miners and he journeyed to Virginia City, Montana, where he sold out. The sale of that first wagonload gave him his first bankroll, which he proceeded to build into a fortune.

From there, he moved on to Nebraska City, Nebraska, where he again loaded a wagon train with supplies. But this time he shipped them by steamer up the Missouri River to Helena, Montana. There he opened a store that he operated until 1890. Murphy was one of the leading cattle ranchers in Montana and president of the Helena National Bank. He also invested heavily and profitably in various mining operations and sheep ranches.

In 1871, he married Elizabeth T. Morton of Clay County, Missouri. They had four children: William M., Frances D., Addie M. and John T. Jr.

When his first wife died in 1897, he married Clara Cobb from Providence, Rhode Island, whom he met while vacationing in Florida.

Born June 28, 1839, in Tecumseh, Michigan, Thomas Burroughs was educated and lived there until the Civil War when he enlisted in Company G of the Michigan Volunteer Cavalry. He was wounded and received an honorable discharge. Returning to Michigan, he remained only a short time before moving to Ames, Iowa.

In 1869, he moved to Cherokee County where he bought land and began raising cattle. Over the years, his land and cattle holdings grew to be extensive. Burroughs also invested in the Scribner Fulton Bank, which was operated as the Scribner Burroughs Bank until 1903 when the name was changed to the First National Bank. He was responsible for securing the Sioux Falls and Omaha lines of the Illinois Central Railroad in Cherokee as well as a state hospital. He also invested in land in Mississippi and in 1903 moved to Chicago. In 1871, he married Adeline Phipps and the couple had four children. He died in 1932 at his home in Chicago, but was buried in Cherokee, Iowa.

Born near Fort Scott, Kansas, Barber grew up and worked as a farmer and nurseryman, carpenter and inventor there. At age thirty, he moved to Chicago to become a partner in a construction business operated by his brother. He was a successful, self-taught architect by the time he moved from Chicago to Knoxville, Tennessee, in 1888. He had a series of partners, but history indicates his most productive partnership was with Thomas A. Kluttz, who joined the firm in 1895.

By 1898, in addition to his architectural practice, Barber had established The American Home Publishing Co., printing sketchbooks of his designs for residences, storefronts, barns and summer houses as well as a monthly magazine titled *The American Home*.

Barber's house kit was so successful that Sears and Roebuck later used it. Barber houses were built in every state and in Japan and China. Today dozens of his houses have been listed on the National Register of Historic Homes.

After marrying, Barber had two sons, George Jr. and Charles, and a daughter, Laura. He died February 17, 1915, in Knoxville. His son, Charles, also established a reputation as an excellent architect. Today Barber designs are still being built and a fan club composed of owners of Barber houses remains active.

Originally published in a 1990 brochure by Prudy's Press.

Happy New Year Happy New Century 1900

New Year's Eve 1899 was a very special time for the residents of Fort Myers. Around eleven o'clock on New Year's Eve, the townspeople gathered downtown at the corner of First and Hendry Streets. Church bells pealed, as the *Fort Myers Press* reported, to honor the dying century.

At midnight, whistles, firecrackers, pistols, rifles, shotguns and even a cannon blasted the night air. At the Seminole Canning Plant over on Lee Street, the whistle was tied back so that it would remain open and vocal. The steamship, *H.B. Plant* was anchored at the city dock in the Caloosahatchee River and the captain cut loose with the ship's whistle.

Men and young boys formed an impromptu procession behind a local band consisting of drums and fifes and paraded up and down unpaved First Street. Afterward, the men surged into Gilbert's Oyster Saloon to toast the newborn century.

The final decade of the nineteenth century had been difficult. Many major events had taken place that, while not necessarily negative, had been unsettling and had changed both the business and social climate of the area. The killer freeze in 1894, for example, had decimated the truck farmers. Fields of tomatoes, eggplant, peppers, cabbages—the crops planted for the winter market—were blackened by the frost and decayed in the sun. On the other hand, Lee County's citrus crop was not damaged, but fewer than a hundred acres of citrus had been planted. The fruit from those trees sold at exorbitant prices and this changed the face of the local citrus industry as growers from central Florida began moving into Lee County where frost damage to citrus was less severe.

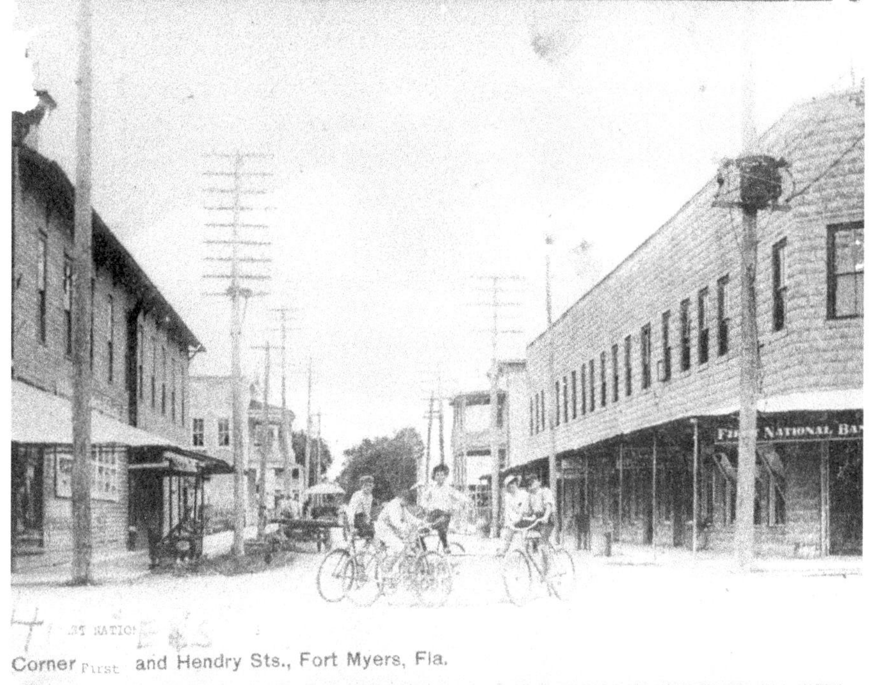

Downtown Fort Myers at the corner of First and Hendry Streets at the turn of the century. *Courtesy of Southwest Florida Historical Museum.*

The Spanish-American War, which erupted in 1898, had also brought change to the area—a blessing to local cattlemen and to Florida's cattle industry. Once the U.S. Army occupied Cuba, the demand for beef was so strong that Lee County cattle brought top dollar and the ranges were soon almost bare. Local cowhands were hired to scour the state for additional herds and Punta Rassa was once again an active port as these cattle were shipped from Punta Rassa to Havana.

The new year was only two days old when a significant event in Lee County's history occurred. On January 2, 1900, Gilmer M. Heitman approached the county commissioners seeking a franchise to establish and operate a telephone company. A fourteen-year franchise was granted and on Wednesday, February 21, 1900, the Lee County Telephone Company's first operator, Mrs. Alice Tooke McCann, was at the switchboard and on official duty in the company's headquarters on the second floor of the Heitman Building at the corner of First and Jackson Streets. Several months later the lines were expanded to reach Buckingham; the following year to Naples and by 1904, Lee County residents could actually call Tampa.

The population of Fort Myers had reached an all-time high of 943. Lee Countians numbered 3,071. Florida's entire population numbered only slightly more than a half million.

In 1900, Fort Myers was not quite fifteen years old as an incorporated city and Lee County was not quite thirteen. Transportation was still mainly by water for the railroad had not yet come to town and there were no paved roads into the area. It's interesting to note what Fort Myers did *not* have as the new century dawned: the city did not have a hospital, a fire department, a municipal waterworks, an ice plant, a public library or paved streets. Yet while Fort Myers was transformed in the twentieth century, those people who celebrated New Year's Eve in downtown Fort Myers in 1999 would have recognized it because, fortunately, much remains the same.

Originally published in the special Lee County 2000 Edition of Lee Living.

Dean Park
1900

Officially known as Dean's Subdivision but more commonly referred to as Dean Park, this subdivision is best described as a pocket of local history. In its time, Dean Park was one of the most exclusive developments in Fort Myers, but parts of it also served as a place for sandlot baseball and as a local lovers' lane.

Its residents included leaders in the community. One of these was Miss Flossie Hill. One of the area's very first businesswomen, "Miss Flossie" owned a dress shop on First Street in downtown Fort Myers for many years. She lived in a home on the banks of Billy's Creek. John Morgan Dean, the developer, lived in the two-story cypress shingle home built in 1907 at the corner of First Street (now Palm Beach Boulevard) and Avalon. Most of its homes were built between 1900 and 1925 and many of its residents are descendants of pioneer families.

Just down the street toward town are the former Alderman and Chadwick Homes. Frank Alderman Sr. was a local attorney who was very active in both the legal and banking communities. For a number of years, he was chairman of the Board of Directors of the First National Bank (at the time of this writing C&S Bank). Clarence A.Chadwick, who invented safety paper for the printing of bank checks, came to the area in 1923 and was active in local real estate as well as the citrus industry where he specialized in limes. Chadwick owned a great deal of land on Captiva and is the man for whom Chadwick's Restaurant at South Seas Plantation is named.

Other families living in Dean Park area included the Harry Stuckeys, the Virgil Robbs and the Ted Evanses. Charlie Powell, Dean's nephew, still lives there, as does Mrs. Vernon Widerquist. Widerquist served as one of Fort Myers's first city commissioners and later as mayor. Directly across the street from the former Dean home, which is located at 2582 First Street, are the former Lozier and Heitman homes. Lozier, an automobile manufacturer, built his home on the Caloosahatchee River in 1914. Next door at 1583 First Street is the Gilmer Heitman Sr. home built in 1908.

Dean Park is irregular in shape, bounded by the Caloosahatchee River on one side, Michigan Avenue to the south, Billy's Creek and Palm Avenue to the east and Evans Avenue for a portion of the west. The subdivision was named after its developer, John Morgan Dean, who built the Morgan Hotel (now known as the Dean Hotel) in downtown Fort Myers. Dean Street was named after him as well.

Lee County Clerk of Courts J.W. Garner officially accepted the plat for Dean's Subdivision in May of 1924, but many of the homes were already standing. Dean, who had come to Fort Myers for the first time in 1898 to hunt, purchased the thirty-eight acres destined to become Dean Park in 1901 from Peck Brothers of Chicago. He paid $8,500. In 1911, he began the development work, which entailed a great deal of fill for the land was very low and swampy. William W. Montgomery operated the dredge for Dean and, according to Montgomery's granddaughter, Sandra Winslow, worked for him for many years on other projects.

Two major streets within the development are Providence and Rhode Island. The selection of those names was neither coincidental nor accidental. Dean, who was born in Worcester, Massachusetts, had started his career in Providence, where he was in the furniture business. Rhode Island Avenue during the height of the real estate boom was familiarly known as "Millionaire's Row."

But not everyone remembers Dean Park as an exclusive subdivision. Former Sheriff Snag Thompson remembers it as a ballpark. "We called it Dean Park Fill," Thompson recalls. "There wasn't a single house from the Elks Club (today it's the American Legion Home) and Billy's Creek was vacant. And we had sandlot football and sandlot baseball, Angus and Walter Grace and my brother Carlton and me and Charlie Powell played baseball and football out there."

Thompson chuckles. "We had hand-me-downs, but we wouldn't let Gilmer [Heitman Jr.] play with us because Gilmer had silk stuff his daddy'd bought him right out of Saks Fifth Avenue."

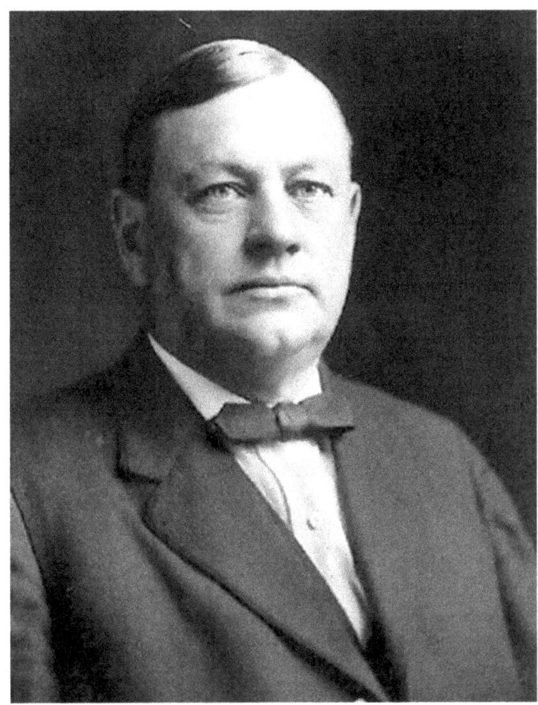

John Dean, developer of Dean Park. *Courtesy of Rhoda Hopson Ingram.*

Thompson, decorated for bravery several times, later ran into Heitman in Italy during World War II, where Heitman lived down his reputation (at least in Thompson's eyes) of being a sissy. Thompson says earnestly, "He really proved himself to be a man."

And returning to the subject of Dean Park Fill, it had still another use. "That's where all of us young people used to park with our girlfriends. There and down where the Boulevard Shopping Center is."

In the 1920s, Dean Park was in its heyday. Fort Myers was growing rapidly to the east, where the only bridge crossed the Caloosahatchee at Freemont Street. At its peak, East Fort Myers had incorporated, had its own police chief, fire chief, mayor, city council—even its own bank.

But several things changed the path of Fort Myers's growth, affecting Dean Park as well. The location of the Edison Bridge at the foot of Fowler Street rather than Fremont Street (which the consultant had recommended) was one of the most devastating developments. Despite this, residents voted to be incorporated into Fort Myers proper because of lower taxes and the need for more city services. Growth had continued although the community's bright future had dimmed when the bank failed and real estate values plummeted during the real estate bust. However, the relocation of the Edison Bridge and its opening in 1931 marked the end of East Fort Myers's growth surge.

Today, a committee composed of its residents is working to have Dean Park declared a national historic district, battling to preserve the community with its charming architecture which represents a very significant period in Fort Myers's growth and development. Jeanie Gibson and Dinesh Sharma are co-chairs.

According to Gibson, the movement began as the formation of a neighborhood association several years ago. "We organized to revitalize the neighborhood, to prevent it from deteriorating any further," she said.

Once the association was formed, Neighborhood Watch was reactivated and residents pitched in to clean vacant lots and encourage others to take care of and upgrade their homes.

Detractors of the idea of declaring Dean Park a historic district maintain that it's a high crime area, but according to Fort Myers Police Chief Jere Spurlin that's just not so. "Due to its geographical location it probably has more [crime] than some areas along McGregor Boulevard, but not by any stretch of the imagination is it a high crime area," Spurlin says. "To me, I would consider it to be an average area of the city from the standpoint of crime."

Gibson says the committee is presently working to compile a history of the area. Once that's done, they'll propose to the state that Dean Park be nominated for the State Registry of Historic Neighborhoods.

UPDATE: Dean Park received its historical designation in 1997. Today the old homes and estates are being restored and Dean Park is once again one of the most prestigious developments in Fort Myers.

Originally published in the June 1, 1986 edition of the Fort Myers News-Press.

A Pioneer's Thanksgiving 1909

The roar of football fans and the resonant voices of sports announcers will filter through television sets to enliven the living rooms of homes in southwest Florida this Thanksgiving. An occasional automobile will drive past on the paved streets of our cities. Overhead jets landing at and taking off from the Southwest Florida Regional Airport will leave their trails of vapor to drift like fleecy clouds against the backdrop of our vivid blue skies.

How different that is from Thanksgiving seventy-five years ago. Then the streets were wide, grassy lanes. Women cooked on wood stoves; microwave ovens were not yet even an idea. The aviation industry was in its infancy and Orville Wright had set a new record by remaining aloft one hour, one minute and forty seconds while carrying a passenger.

Automobiles were such a novelty that the *Fort Myers Press* ran a front-page story about the formation of a local auto club, and everyone who owned a car was invited to join. The first car had appeared in Fort Myers a little more than a year earlier, in September 1908.

From a national point of view, 1909 had seen significant developments: The National Association for the Advancement of Colored People had been formed; the Sixteenth Amendment to the U.S. Constitution had been submitted to the states for ratification providing for the levying of an income tax; and Robert E. Peary had discovered the North Pole.

Locally, Fort Myers was enjoying its first moving picture theatre. The buildings along First Street were largely frame. Fort Myers was approaching a population of 2,500 and a person could buy twenty acres of land, including four acres of grove, for $800. The real estate business was becoming so important that the *Press* announced it was going to have a page devoted to sales and transactions and urged real estate people to bring their news to the paper's office.

The Bank of Fort Myers, which had been formed several years earlier, listed capital in excess of $75,000 and resources of $250,000. John Trice was the president, and the other officers had familiar names: Harvie E. Heitman was vice president, J.E. Foxworthy was cashier and J.E. Hendry Jr. was assistant cashier.

One of the lead stories on the front page of the *Press* was headlined, "Thanksgiving at Marco...A Royal Feast Was Spread," which recounted a Florida holiday with a community Thanksgiving program at the Marco school, followed by a picnic at the beach.

The schoolhouse was "transformed into a veritable fairy bower" by Miss Lettie Nutt, the schoolteacher who had arrived that September. It was decorated with "products of grove and garden, field and wood—a center group of pineapples, [pine] cones, and berries. Corn and cotton were suspended from about the table," as were drawings by the students and printed Bible verses appropriate to the day.

The program began "when the gramophone sounded the opening number," which was followed by a march and the pupils filed in from opposite side doors, creating a charming tableau as they crossed in front of the audience and took their places on the platform.

The complete program was not printed, although the *Press* reported, "Little children and more mature pupils acquitted themselves most creditably." After the program at Marco Beach was held, the reporter enthused that "the picnickers found themselves possessed of sharp appetites and were glad to obey the call to dinner. Even 43 sharp appetites proved unequal in disposing of the abundance of dainties under which the tables fairly groaned."

The menu ranged from "meats and poultry, chicken pie, turkey, chicken with rice, roast chicken...and there must have been another kind for a two year old was heard begging for 'some more rooster' to jams and jellies and salads to raisin pie, peach pie, apricot pie, and cakes."

Still another kind of party was reported on the front page, and this was just as traditional: a hunting party. "This week," the article read, "a party of Alabama people went out under the guidance of Adolphus Carson and Sam Thompson and succeeded in bagging 10 deer, 13 turkey, 5 wildcats and 4 rattlesnakes, besides all the small game the camp could use." The party was hunting in the vicinity of Crow's Nest and Devil's Garden in what was then south Lee County.

The article was a roundup of various hunting parties and described by local guide Dave Pool. "A remarkable feature about this was that the doctor (Dr. A.B. Brown, one of the party) had never seen a deer before in the woods and with his very first shot brought him down."

Much as some merchants still do today, W.B. Winkler ran an ad thanking the people in town for their patronage at his drug store. Fort Myers was looking forward to having "electric lights go on for the entire night" and to a city council meeting the next day, which promised "some warm questions to come up."

Originally published in "Only Yesterday" in the November 11, 1984 edition of the Fort Myers News-Press.

Lofton's Island
1910

Desolate...violated by vandals...visited only by egrets, cranes and wood storks...Lofton's Island is a haven of memories. It echoes with the giggles of a schoolgirl who swam with her pet deer, the soft laughter of that same girl as a bride and with the muted grief of a widow from a different generation.

Now the play of breezes through the Australian pines and the flapping wings and cries of the birds that have taken it for a home, are the island's sounds. Of course, you can hear the jets overhead and the roar of cars on the bridges, but they don't intrude upon the island's air of isolation.

The island was created from spoil in 1910 when the river was dredged to form a turning basin for steamers such as the *Mildred*, the *City of Philadelphia* and the *H.B. Plant.*

J.L. Lofton, then in the dredging business, recognized its possibilities as a home site and homesteaded it. In 1911, he and his wife, Florence, and their seven-year old daughter, Zelma, moved into the three-bedroom frame house he'd built there. His daughter, now Mrs. H.F. Kuester, remembers her childhood.

> *At first it was so different from living in town. I didn't have many playmates so Daddy got the Indians to catch a buck deer for me to play with. Later, Thomas Edison saw my father around town and said he had a doe that was eating up all his shrubbery and asked if Daddy'd like to have it for his little girl. Daddy said yes. At one time, I had five pet deer...*

I also tamed a couple of pelicans in my spare time, but they got to be terrible pests. I had a pet rabbit, too. It came to me on a clump of hyacinths after a storm and stayed a while but then left—by the same method, I guess...

We had gaslights and a small carbide gas stove although we mostly used a kerosene stove for cooking. And we had an iron that was heated by gas, but I don't think it ever worked right...

The house was built six feet off the ground and we had a place under there where we did the laundry. We had a rainwater tank and several large tubs. But this was a lot of trouble and later we just sent it out...

Once a week we'd go into town for groceries. We had a great big icebox so Daddy'd buy a 100-pound block of ice and bring it back on the bow of the boat. Every day I rowed across the river to town to go to school. I'd tie up at the dock, and walk to the school, which was in the bungalow on Royal Palm Avenue. Later when I was older, Daddy got me a launch. Saturdays Dad would pick up my friends at the dock and bring them over to spend the day with me...

I even met my husband on the island. He came over to see the deer.

Her husband, Harold F. Kuester, explained their meeting. He said,

My dad had a paint shop at the end of Ireland's dock...it was pretty high off the water. I used to do a lot of fishing and hunting. I looked over one day when I was fishing on the dock and saw the deer on the island. So a little later I just got into my boat and rowed over there. I met Pete [his nickname for Mrs. Kuester] *and we were married there in 1924...*

Joe Ansley's father, he was the Baptist minister, performed the ceremony for us. Got up out of a sickbed to do it. I think we were one of the last couples [he] *married.*

In the early part of 1929, Lofton sold the island to Tom Phillips for $4,000. Phillips, a real estate developer, had a plat of the island recorded, which laid it out in a subdivision of twenty 100-by-160-foot lots. At this point, purchase of the island carried with it the right to connect onto the Edison Bridge and to fill within one inch of the bridge. This permission has since been revoked.

Phillips was inactive during the Depression and his plans for developing the island remained unrealized. Then, in 1950, A. Lowell Hunt, author of *Florida Today*, and his wife, Elinor, who were then living on Sanibel, purchased

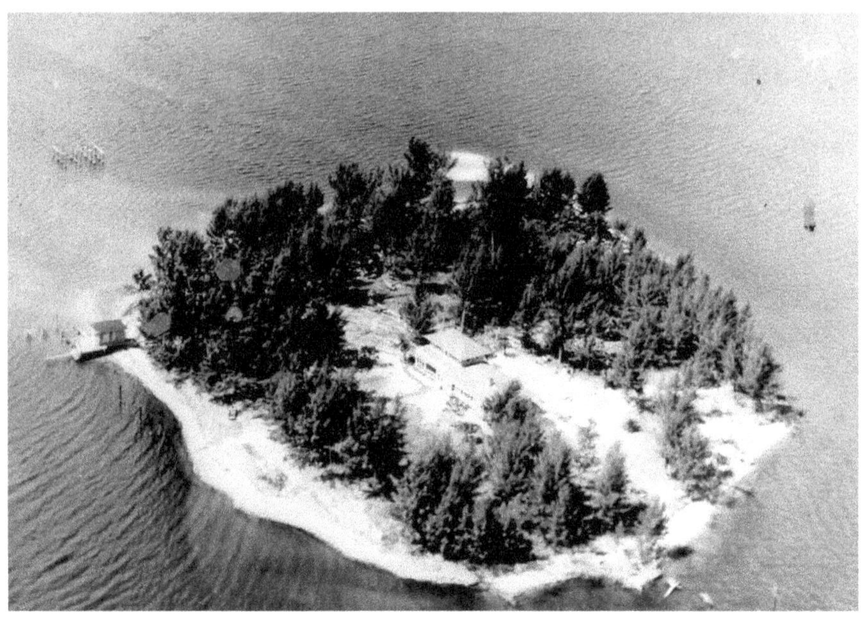

The home in the center of Lofton's Island is the home that was built by author A. Lowell Hunt and his wife Elinor in 1950. *Courtesy of Mrs. Elinor Hunt.*

the island from Phillips for $8,000. They built a seven-room, three-bath frame house from materials taken to the island in Hunt's fourteen-foot outboard skiff. Mrs. Hunt says,

> *My husband was kind of an adventurer and the idea of living on the island appealed to him strongly. We looked at other places, but fell in love with the island. We moved onto the island in 1951. It was very peaceful, remote. We didn't go by clocks very much—we could always tell when it was 10 o'clock and 5 o'clock by the boats passing on the river.*

The Hunts found life on the island still as serene, but much easier than the Loftons had, because Florida Power and Light brought an underwater power cable to the island so they had electricity for lighting, cooking and refrigeration. But their lighting system had one hazard not common to the average homeowner: alligators.

In fact, one alligator ate the insulation of the marine cable, which resulted in a temporary loss of power. The trouble crew investigating the scene found the culprit's body wrapped in the cable. They never determined, however, whether it was electrocution or indigestion that caused the denizen's untimely demise.

In 1961, Hunt died on the island and shortly after, Mrs. Hunt moved to the mainland. In 1963, it was again the focus of public interest when it was proposed as a site for a "tower of light." Designed as a tourist attraction and memorial to Thomas A. Edison, plans were to fill the island to provide parking for ten thousand cars and to connect onto the bridge for access. Financial and community support were lacking, however, and the project never advanced beyond the planning stage.

Now the property of sisters Mara Shkil and Dorothy Akers, who live in North Fort Myers but are spending the summer in Cleveland, Ohio, Lofton's Island waits, drowsing in the sun, for the next chapter of its history to unfold.

Originally published in the July 6, 1969 edition of the Fort Myers News-Press.

A Friend Gone: Tootie McGregor Terry 1912

In earlier years, bad news always arrived by telegram. The unfamiliar yellow envelope with the clear inset where the address was revealed was, for most people, a dreaded correspondence.

The news that H.E. Heitman received in the form of a telegram on the morning of August 17, 1912, was no exception. It contained the "sad intelligence," as the *Fort Myers Press* was to write, that Tootie McGregor Terry had died at her summer home at Mamaroneck-on-the-Hudson in New York.

The respect and affection that the city of Fort Myers felt for its benefactress was well documented in an editorial published on the day of her funeral in Cleveland, Ohio. One unmistakable measure of that affection was revealed by the fact that Heitman kept his store closed the Saturday of her death and that all the stores in downtown Fort Myers had closed for three hours during her funeral.

The affection and respect were well earned. The *Press* reported that Tootie McGregor Terry owned both the Royal Palm and the Riverview hotels and had financed Harvey Heitman in the construction of the Bradford Hotel, which was named after her son.

Early in 1912, Mrs. Terry had offered to construct the twenty-mile portion of McGregor Boulevard from Whiskey Creek to Punta Rassa and to pay $500 a year for its upkeep for five years, providing the city built a boulevard from Monroe Street to the creek.

In the *Fort Myers Press* editorial on the day of her funeral—which was headlined "A Friend Gone"—the writer concluded, "Fort Myers and Lee

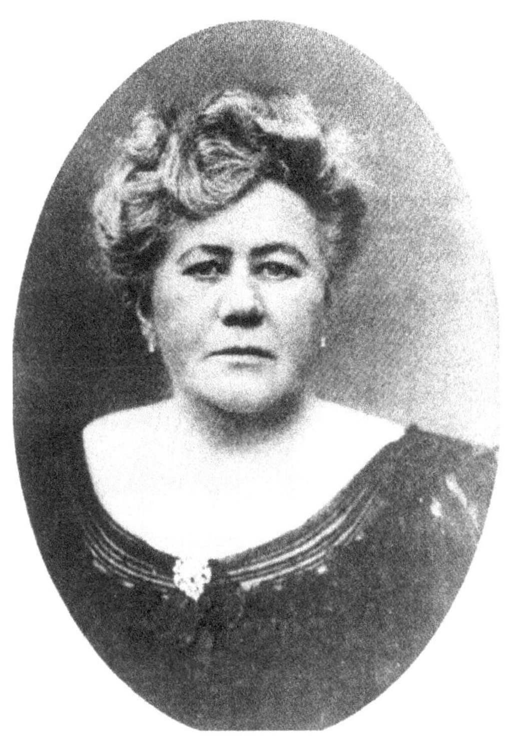

Tootie McGregor Terry. *Courtesy of Southwest Florida Historical Museum.*

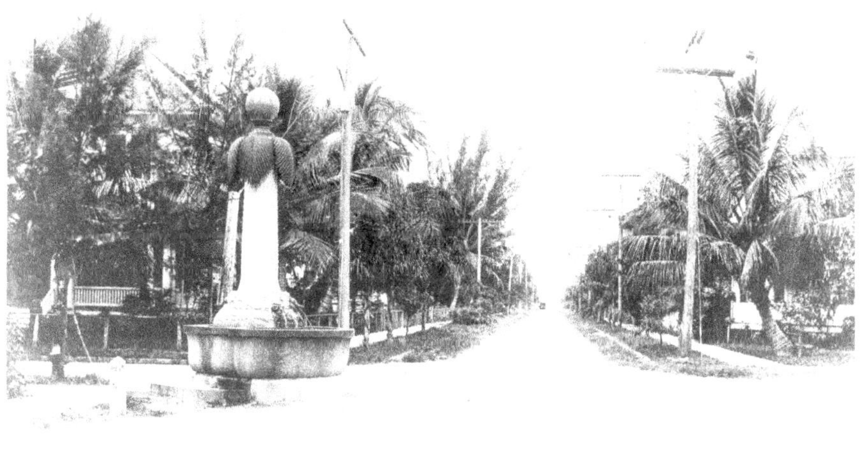

The Tootie McGregor memorial fountain in its original location. *Courtesy of Southwest Florida Historical Museum.*

County has [*sic*] lost a good, true friend, and the place vacated will be one hard to fill."

Assured by her widower, Dr. Marshall Orlando Terry (former U.S. surgeon general), that he would honor his wife's commitment to McGregor Boulevard, Fort Myers continued work on the road, which was named to honor Tootie's first husband, Ambrose McGregor, a major stockholder in Standard Oil.

Karl Grismer wrote that by the summer of 1914, a macadam road was completed to Whiskey Creek. "Difficulties encountered by Dr. Terry in settling his wife's estate prevented him from proceeding as rapidly as he had expected," Grismer wrote, "but by the summer of 1915 he had completed it, with bridges and culverts, at a cost of $105,000. The county commissioners formally accepted the boulevard...on July 14, 1915."

On December 6, 1912, the Fort Myers City Council read a letter from Dr. Terry in which he proposed to build a memorial fountain for his late wife in Fort Myers, provided the city would meet certain conditions. The acceptance resolution stated these terms.

> *Be it resolved by the city council that we hereby bind said city, our successors in office...to light said fountain with not less than five incandescent electric lights of 32 candlepower each, and that water shall always be provided by the city of Fort Myers in sufficient volume for carrying full capacity of its fountain.*

The city also agreed to place the fountain at some "prominent point within the city," approved by both Dr. Terry and the city council. The site decided upon was what old-timers called Five Points, the intersection of Cleveland Avenue, Anderson Avenue (now Dr. Martin Luther King Jr. Boulevard), McGregor Boulevard, and Main and Carson Streets.

The fountain was completed in the summer of 1913. In the July 10, 1913 edition of the *Fort Myers Press*, a reporter noted, "Nearly all the material for the McGregor memorial fountain is in the ground and ready to set in place. Workmen who have been sent here by the designers of this beautiful granite shaft and fountain, have placed the heavier pieces in position for erection which work will be undertaken within the next few days." That, however, is all that was written, other than another a brief notice a week or so later that work was progressing well.

No mention was made of any formal dedication ceremony, nor the fountain's completion, until the next month, when the *Press* observed, "The Terry memorial fountain was draped by a beautiful bouquet of ferns and roses all day Sunday, it being the first anniversary of Mrs. T. McGregor Terry"—the first anniversary of her death.

The fountain stood at Five Points until 1952, when construction of the over-cross to the Caloosahatchee Bridge was begun. It was disassembled, and the marble palm tree that formed the base and central portion of it was moved to the Fort Myers Country Club. The five snakes (two cottonmouth moccasins, two rattlesnakes and a coral snake) that formed the spouts from which the water issued were dismantled and stored.

The monument is currently being restored by Naples sculptor Don Wilkins. According to Wilkins, it is made of pink granite found in northern Georgia. It weights 48,000 pounds and although the price tag was $5,000 when it was built, Wilkins says it would cost at least $250,000 to replace it today.

Wilkins had to replace the monument's coral snake, but it is impossible to discern any difference between it and the other snakes. The city of Fort Myers is once again keeping its word to provide proper lighting, location and water for the monument.

And the words on the statue have as much meaning for Lee County residents today as they did in 1913. On one side of the monument, the simple inscription reads, "Presented to Fort Myers by Dr. Marshall Orlando Terry," but on the other side, Mrs. Terry's words are cited and they read simply, "I only hope the little I have done may be an incentive to others to do more."

Originally published in "Only Yesterday" in the November 25, 1984 edition of the Fort Myers News-Press.

The Birth of a Hospital: Lee Memorial 1916

Telegraph keys in Fort Myers chattered, speeding the message to Dr. Daniel McSwain in Arcadia that Sam Thompson was ill and needed immediate surgery. The year was 1916, and Lee Memorial Hospital had just opened on October 3. And although Thompson's ailment, acute appendicitis, is not necessarily a life threatening illness now, it was sixty-nine years ago. Time became an excruciatingly important factor since McSwain had to travel by train approximately fifty miles from Arcadia to Fort Myers.

Dr. McSwain caught the next train and traveled overnight, arriving the next morning and operating successfully. This surgery is significant since it was the first operation performed at Lee Memorial Hospital. However, it also provides an indication of how primitive facilities were here, for Nursing Superintendent Edith Davidson had to go to Dr. G.F. Henry's office in downtown Fort Myers to sterilize the bandages.

Located at the corner of Victoria and Grand avenues, this new hospital was not the first established here. Its progenitor was an army hospital built at the fledgling Fort Myers in the 1850s. The military hospital was surrounded in controversy for it cost $30,000 to construct, at that time an exorbitant figure, which resulted in a congressional investigation.

While the hospital at the military outpost had been the center of controversy because of its cost, the new Lee Memorial Hospital was also enmeshed in conflict, but from a safer distance. Actually, the real dissension centered on the construction of a new county courthouse—considered reckless extravagance by a conservative element in the community.

Today it's surprising to realize that Fort Myers did not have a hospital. Incorporated for almost thirty years, the young town was growing in population. Furthermore, if someone became seriously ill there were three options, none of which was efficient. The patient could either be transported by boat to Key West or Tampa or treated at his or her home. The Tamiami Trail hadn't been built and roads were literally wagon ruts. However, people were concerned and aware of the need. As early as January 1912, a group of citizens had gathered to discuss the problem. A committee had been formed and headed by Mayor L.A. Hendry and Dr. J.E. Brecht, president of the medical society, and composed of representatives of local churches and civic organizations. The Fort Myers City Council voted to provide $300, but no further progress was made until the old frame courthouse was torn down to be replaced by a modern yellow brick edifice. The thrifty wrecking crew that tore down the old courthouse, appreciating their difficult position, carefully salvaged the lumber and created neat piles of wood, which were later used to build the hospital.

Karl Grismer writes, "Many still believed that a hospital was just a place to die in, and since they did not care about dying they did not care about a hospital. Even some of the physicians were apathetic and a few were openly antagonistic."

The donation of the lumber by the county to the city, however, put new zest into the drive for the hospital. An anonymous donor gave land for the

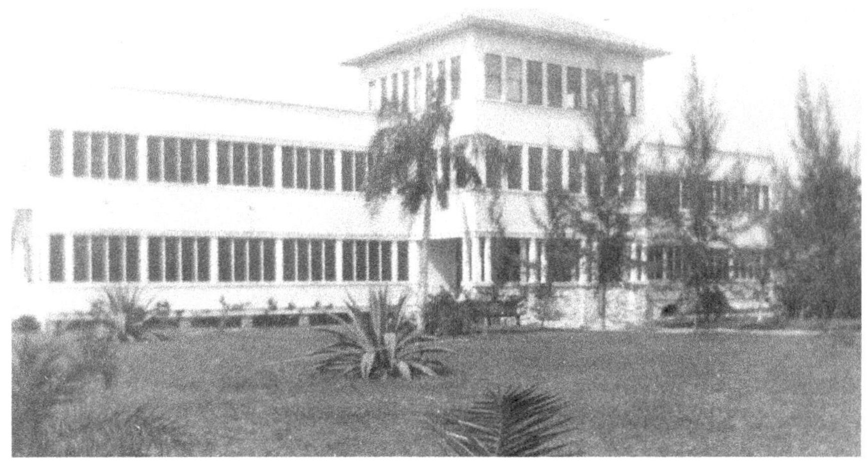

The original Robert E. Lee Memorial Hospital, shown here in the 1920s. *Courtesy of Southwest Florida Historical Museum.*

building on the south side of town on the corner of Grand Avenue and Victoria Street. Other donations came; but they trickled in.

The *Fort Myers News-Press* reported in its February 1, 1950 Centennial Edition (the fort was one hundred years old) that when the original Lee Memorial Hospital opened, "The grounds were desolate, with no grass, no shrubs, and...[the hospital was] surrounded by the Negro section."

The United Daughters of the Confederacy had worked hard to raise money for the new hospital; so when they requested it be named the Robert E. Lee Memorial Hospital, the hospital board listened. Over the years, the name was shortened to Lee Memorial Hospital.

Lee Memorial Hospital was small. A square, two-story building with screened porches along the front on both floors, it had four rooms for patients and an operating room, but no delivery room, so babies were delivered in the mothers' rooms. With no elevator, patients were carried by hand from the second-floor operating room downstairs to their rooms on the first floor. Patients didn't worry as much about the skill of the surgeon as they did about the surefootedness of the orderlies carrying them from the operating room to their beds. Recovery rooms were unheard of at the time.

During the next twenty-five years there were two additions. In the early 1930s, the hospital created a maternity suite so that new mothers had a separate "reception" room with a rocking chair where they could entertain family and friends who came to see the newborn. And by 1941, the hospital offered sixteen rooms with accommodations for twenty-two patients.

The hospital on Victoria Avenue served the community well, but the town was growing, and in 1939 WPA funds became available to build a new structure. However, as economic conditions improved during World War II, the number of people on the WPA rolls declined and it was difficult to find laborers. Completion of the hospital was further delayed because of the outbreak of World War II with the resultant shortage of materials and even more severe lack of workers. Once the war ended, construction began again.

The new $200,000 Lee Memorial Hospital opened April 18, 1943. On the front page of the *Fort Myers News-Press* that month, which also carried a headline "Moonshine Still Found At Bayshore," another article praised the new hospital with its new operating room done in green tiles as "one of the most modern to be found anywhere."

A couple days earlier, *News-Press* reporter Rufe Daughtrey had been treated to an advance tour of the new facility. He wrote, "That new hospital out on Cleveland Avenue is just about the nicest place imaginable to be sick in. It's got just about everything from magnificent sun decks to a cozy parlor where you can play cards in front of a fire on a chilly evening."

Daughtrey also pointed out the hospital was "front to back" since the entrance on Cleveland Avenue (the main access road) was used strictly for emergencies and ambulances. Regular visitors or patients would drive around to the back to enter.

The grand opening was held Sunday, April 18. More than one thousand people attended, creating a traffic snarl. It was so bad, in fact, that hospital president Harry J. Wood was late for the one brief ceremony in which the Methodist Golden Cross Circle presented a check to furnish a hospital room. That check, incidentally, was in the amount of $210. The cost of furnishing a room was $360 and the Methodist ladies had not yet raised the entire amount. However, Mrs. Frank Bentley, present that day for the ceremonies, stepped forward with a check for $150.

Today Lee Memorial Hospital has soared skyward and groaned sideways. Its multi-million dollar plant dwarfs, overpowers and even consumes the modest building erected with such pride in 1943. Furthermore, the institution has endured turbulent times during the intervening forty-two years, but now seems to once again be growing and serving its community well and with dignity.

> UPDATE: At this writing in August 2005, Lee Memorial Hospital has been named one of the top one hundred hospitals in the country for stroke, orthopedics and its intensive care unit (ICU).

Originally published in "Only Yesterday" in the July 1985 edition of the Fort Myers News-Press.

The Edison Legacy
1884–Present

To the rest of the civilized world, Thomas Alva Edison was an inventor of awesome genius, a citizen of the world made so by the vast brilliance of his mind, which spanned nationalities and the body of heretofore-sacrosanct scientific knowledge.

To the residents of early Fort Myers, Edison was all this and more. Edison was a neighbor, a benefactor, a friend and in all instances, a person who left an imprint on our area still visible today fifty-one years after his death. To see Edison's legacy for yourself, you need not look far. A glance down McGregor Boulevard is an excellent place to begin.

Although Edison was not the first to bring Royal Palm trees to Fort Myers, he was responsible for having them planted along McGregor Boulevard. In 1901, he arranged to have them planted from Monroe Street to Manuel's Drive. The original lot did not survive and had to be replanted three times. Edison is credited both with having those first palms planted and also with the idea.

On the right as you drive down McGregor Boulevard, you will see the Edison Winter Home and, on the left, his laboratory. Both were deeded to the City of Fort Myers in 1947 by Edison's widow, Mrs. Mina Miller Edison.

Edison first visited Fort Myers in the winter of 1885, and then brought Mina Miller Edison (his first wife had died) to the area as a bride in 1886. Edison was impressed with the small village, which then boasted a population of 349 and was the second largest city on the west coast of Florida south of Cedar Keys. (Tampa was the largest.) On that first visit, he stopped at a local real estate office to see what land might be available. In September of 1885, Edison purchased a thirteen-acre site from Samuel Summerlin for $2,750. The home was assembled on its present location during the winter of 1885–86.

Supplies for Edison's laboratory were shipped down early in 1887 and, when he returned in March of that year, Edison began work immediately to construct equipment to provide electric lights for his home. Fort Myers residents were among the first in the nation to witness the scientific marvel of Edison's electric light bulb. It's a matter of record that on Saturday night, March 27, 1887, electric lights blazed at Seminole Lodge and nearly everyone in town found a reason to stop by that evening to see them.

Seminole Lodge, the laboratory and a museum are open to the public year-round, so you can visit there and see for yourself his many inventions including the ticker tape, the movie camera and the phonograph.

Although Edison did not return to Fort Myers until the winter of 1901, he remained interested and active in community affairs. In 1900, for example, when the town's first volunteer fire department was formed, Edison sent $100 of the $800 raised to buy equipment.

He did return in 1901 and each succeeding winter until his death in 1931. That he was an asset to the community is unquestioned today, but he was appreciated then as well. In 1926, a bright young developer, James D. Newton, began a new subdivision on McGregor Boulevard just down from Edison's lab. He named it Edison Park in honor of the inventor and, in the sales brochure, pointed out that residents would have Edison and Henry Ford for neighbors.

Edison Park was and is one of the most prestigious subdivisions in Fort Myers. The entrance is still marked by the statue of an ethereal Grecian maiden pouring water from an urn. It is modeled after the gate in Chestnut Hill, a wealthy suburb of Philadelphia, the city Newton left to come to Fort Myers.

As you follow the gracefully curving streets of Edison Park, you will pass the Thomas A. Edison Congregational Church, which marked its fiftieth anniversary on November 1, 1981. This church is still another example of Edison's legacy to Fort Myers. Shortly after the church was chartered on September 30, 1925, the Edisons donated two of the five lots on which the church is situated and helped support the church financially.

Edison and the founding minister, Reverend O.T. Anderson, were close friends and had many intense philosophical discussions. According to the records of the church, one spring shortly before Edison returned to New

Jersey, he asked Reverend Anderson if he believed trees had any thinking ability. When Mr. Anderson expressed doubt, Edison said no more. However, shortly before he left, he instructed a worker to quietly bury a truckload of fertilizer in his lab garden.

When Edison returned from New Jersey several months later, he invited Mr. Anderson over and together they watched while a worker uncovered the pit of fertilizer. In the pit were feeder roots coming from trees in all directions. This was Edison's argument that plants have the ability to know where to look for food and thus have intelligence.

Unfortunately, Edison died just days before the sanctuary opened for worship in 1931. Mrs. Edison and her sister remained members and staunch supporters of the church until their deaths.

At the same time the subdivision was being developed, Fort Myers was in the throes of massive growth as a result of the land boom and experiencing a serious overcrowding problem in the schools. In 1926, the Fort Myers Board of Public Instruction voted to construct a new grammar school in Edison Park. The cornerstone of the school—still in use as an elementary school today—was laid on March 13, 1926, with Mr. and Mrs. Edison on hand for the ceremonies. In fact, it is believed that Edison planted a Brazilian pepper tree on the grounds, a tree which still shades schoolchildren today.

The school opened on March 20, 1927, and, to mark the occasion, all city schools were closed at noon so students could take part in the ceremonies. The Fort Myers Concert Band provided appropriate music and a local Masons Lodge organized a motorcade from the Elks Club on the Caloosahatchee River (now the American Legion) to the school site. When the first class graduated, Edison was again present for the ceremonies.

The school in its time was as distinguished locally as Edison was nationally, for it had the largest auditorium in town. On its stage were produced Lions' Club Minstrels, dance recitals, little theatre plays, fashion shows, and its grounds were the scene of many fish fries, Halloween carnivals and bazaars. For many years, Edison Park School was the cultural center of Lee County.

The current Edison Community College is not the first, but the second college in Lee County to be named after the inventor. The first, Thomas Alva Edison College, was started by Dr. H.O. and Leila Cunningham in 1940. It was opened for classes in what is now the American Legion Building on East First Street. Following World War II, classes were moved to barracks at Buckingham Air Field in East Lee County. The small proprietary college closed in 1948.

Fourteen years later, the second (Edison Junior College) began classes and in 1965 moved to its permanent campus on an eighty-acre site fronting on College Parkway. In 1971, the name was changed to Edison Community College. Its name is noteworthy for it is the only higher education public institution in Florida named after an individual.

In 1976, when the new Technical Building was dedicated, it was discovered that everything to be taught in that building was the result of one or another of Edison's inventions, even health care technologies. With this in mind, the school approached the Charles Edison Foundation (founded by Edison's sons to honor their father and their brother, Charles. Charles was a former governor of New Jersey who had recently died). As a result, the Foundation provided two busts for the building—one of Charles Edison and one, specially commissioned, of Thomas Edison as a young man.

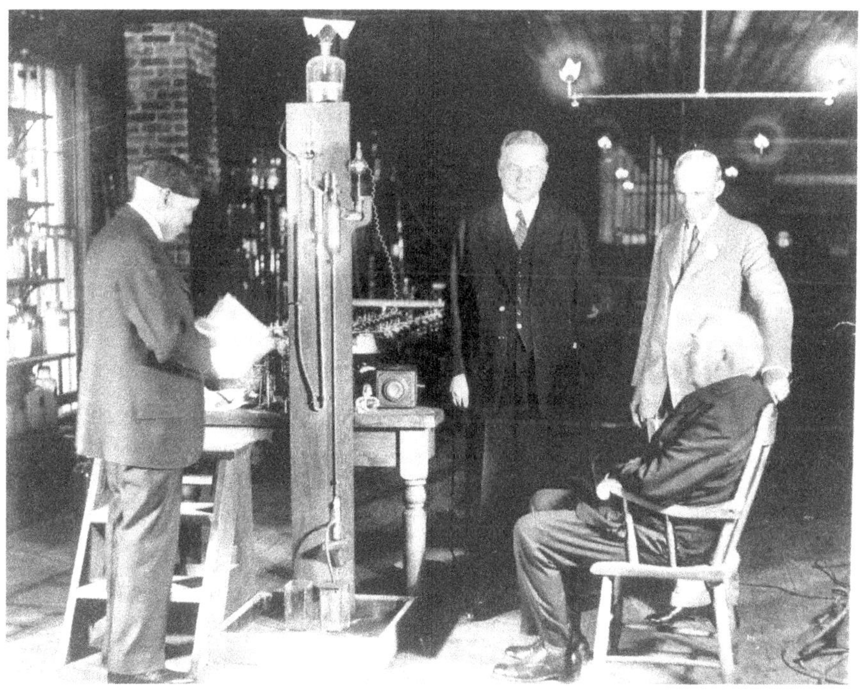

Thomas Alva Edison, shown seated in his Fort Myers laboratory, was a superstar in his era. Even President Herbert Hoover, center, traveled to the small town to visit him on his birthday. Standing next to Edison is Henry Ford. *Courtesy of Southwest Florida Historical Museum.*

Both are on display in the Technical Building. In addition, the Charles Edison Foundation each year funds an electronics engineering technological chair.

Now we come to the area's most popular, best known and certainly most festive memorial to Mr. Edison: the Pageant of Light, held each February.

The first Pageant of Light was held in 1938, lasted three days and featured a coronation ball for members of the newly formed Court of Edisonia, which supplanted the Sunshine Court. It has been held annually since, except during the World War II years. Resumed in 1946, it has grown steadily and now is a two-week festival featuring parades with bands coming from all around the United States and Canada, a birthday party, a round of balls, strolling flower shows, art exhibits, shell shows along with golf, tennis, card and shuffleboard tournaments. It draws several hundred thousand visitors each year and that number is constantly increasing.

Other reminders of Edison abound in Fort Myers for observant people. It's fun to see just how many you can find.

Originally published in 1982 issue of the Fort Myers Resort Area Magazine
by the Fort Myers Chamber of Commerce.

Seminole Lodge
1884

Seminole Lodge is a house of firsts. It was one of the first prefabricated homes in this country and it was among the first homes in the nation to be lighted by electricity.

Fort Myers was just a village with a population of 349 when Edison first visited here in March of 1885. During that first visit which lasted four days, Edison and his business partner, Ezra L. Gilliland, bought the thirteen-acre tract of land where the Edison home and laboratory is situated today.

The yellow frame house, trimmed in white, was the first to be erected on the grounds. Constructed of Florida pine, it is nicknamed the honeymoon cottage by tour guides for it was to this home Edison brought his second wife, Mina Miller, after their marriage in 1886.

However, according to local author Florence Fritz's book titled *Bamboo and Sailing Ships*, as early as July of 1885, Edison, in his correspondence, was already busily designing his permanent home, which he called Seminole Lodge. He and Gilliland had a Boston architect draw plans that, in Edison's words, "reduced to a paper reality" the duplicate homes he and Gilliland would build on their land.

Once the plans were completed, he sent them to Philip Nye, a builder in Fairfield, Maine. Nye purchased a sufficient supply of clear spruce and built the two homes. The houses were shipped in sections to Fort Myers aboard four schooners and assembled here during the winter of 1885 by Eli Thompson and a crew of carpenters. The two homes, since joined and now considered as the Edison winter home, were among the first prefabricated houses in the nation.

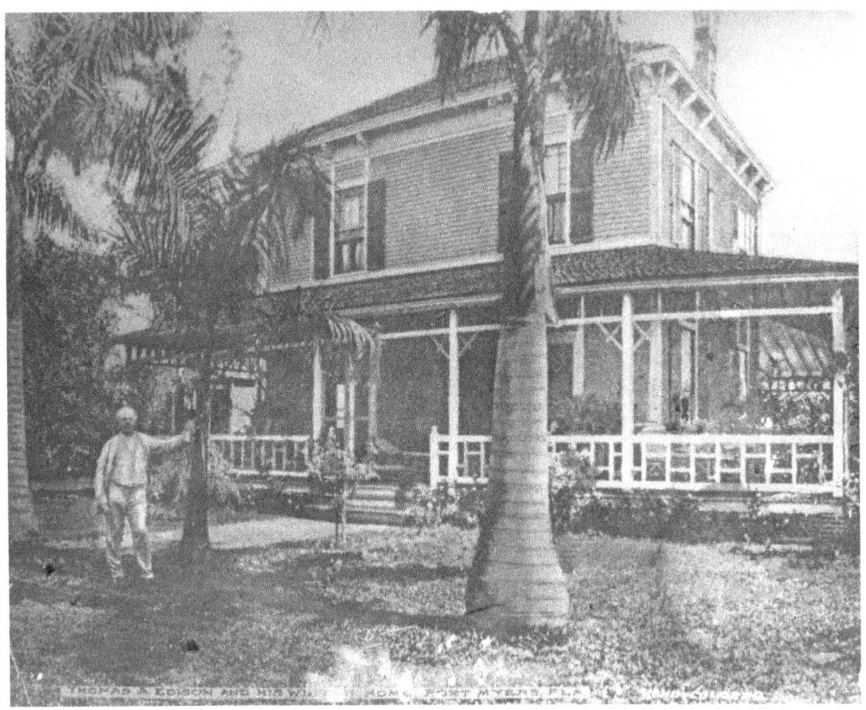

Thomas Alva Edison leans against a royal palm on the grounds of his new home, which he named Seminole Lodge. *Courtesy of Southwest Florida Historical Museum.*

In 1891, Gilliland sold his home and land to Ambrose and Tootie McGregor and the McGregors lived there until 1902 when then-widowed Mrs. McGregor sold it to R.I.O. Travers. In 1906, Mina Edison bought the house and grounds from Travers and subsequently a screened portico was built to unite the two homes.

The Edisons used the first floor of the Gilliland house as a dining room and a game room. Beyond the dining room and across a narrow corridor was the kitchen and butler's pantry. Guests were housed overhead on the second floor, which contained two bedrooms, a sitting room and a bath. The toilet in the guest bath is unique for it had a push button as opposed to a chain pull or lever. The servants were housed over the kitchen.

As you cross the verandah of Edison's original home, you find the master suite on the left. Decorated much as it was then—all the furniture on display is the original furniture—it features wallpaper with the small floral patterns popular then and a lot of white, which was used because it was cooler. On the second floor is another, smaller bedroom which has been nicknamed the doghouse. Across the narrow, open corridor is the main house, which contains the living room and the parlor. The houses are exact, but mirror duplicates which means that the second floor of the main house is also composed of two bedrooms, a sitting room and a bath.

Both houses remain as built with the exception of minor alterations. For example, in the main house, Edison had a small hobby room adjacent to the parlor where he kept models of his various inventions and a telegraph key, for he had been a telegrapher early in his career. Eventually, Mina Edison remodeled this, turning it into a powder room.

Both sections are surrounded by fourteen-foot verandahs that protect the many French doors from the driving rains so common during the rainy season. These verandahs are one of several features of the overall design that made Seminole Lodge extremely practical for life in the semi-tropics.

Phil Warren, local architect and energy analyst with the engineering firm of Burges & O'Neal, praises the design saying, "The large overhangs, the French doors, the high ceilings were the really practical way to build in Florida in the late nineteenth century. They are fine examples of homes built to fit the tropical climate before the days of air conditioning."

In addition to the pleasant, open-air atmosphere, the Edison home is filled with memorabilia and furniture from his era. The furniture is the original and includes much Early American made of mahogany. Wicker furniture was also used both for the verandahs and for the parlors and sitting room. Each of the buildings was heated by a wood-burning fireplace although the kitchen, modernized over the years, contains both an electric and gas stove.

The walls are covered with portraits of the Edisons and hand-painted plates that are now collectors' pieces, not to mention the stuffed owls, pelicans and herons that speak to Mina Edison's love of birds.

The Edison home is a remnant from America's past; not just Florida's, but America's. The piano in the parlor, the bookshelves with the hundreds of well-loved and well-read books, the small desks in the guest rooms so that visitors could write to their families while away from home; all are mute evidence of what life was like then—and how vividly it contrasts to life today.

One fact of life in southwest Florida that remains constant is the interest in gardening, and Edison's gardens are a constant source of pleasure and discovery, for he imported some of the most intriguing trees and shrubs the world has to offer. These are carefully tended by a staff of seven groundskeepers.

Most of the plants and shrubs were selected for practical purposes and played important roles in Edison's research. In fact, the climate and ideal growing conditions were two of Edison's reasons for choosing Fort Myers as a winter home. On display in the laboratory is a piece of rubber made from goldenrod Edison grew on the grounds.

Searching for a filament for his light bulb, he discovered bamboo fibers were sturdier and longer lasting than any other material he had tried, so he eventually grew and tested six thousand varieties before settling on a common Japanese strain.

Edison, a visionary as well as inventor, made many pithy and lasting comments about the world and its future. In our area, he is perhaps best remembered for his prediction that ninety million people were going to discover Fort Myers. Last year, according to Robert Halgrim, curator of the Edison Home & Laboratory Museum, more than 260,000 people visited his home and in the thirty-five years since it was opened to the public nearly three million have toured the house and gardens.

Originally published in the March/April 1982 issue of Home & Condo.

The Awesome Threesome 1916

It was without question Edison's friendship that drew both Henry Ford and Harvey Firestone to Fort Myers. But it was a project shared by the three that added meaning and stimulation to Edison's last years, a project that could have had significant impact on the auto industry.

Ford had long been an ardent admirer of Edison, even prior to their first meeting at a convention in the Oriental Hotel at Manhattan Beach on Long Island in 1891. Ford's biographers have pointed out many different influences Edison had on Ford's life and decisions. Edison, for example, was convinced that cigarette smoking was not healthy and he refused to hire anyone who smoked. Ford followed his lead.

As John Cote Dahlinger relates in his book, *The Secret Life of Henry Ford*, "He wooed the friendship of Edison and almost lived in his shadow." In fact, in 1916 he bought a winter home in Fort Myers immediately adjacent to Edison's. (That home is open to the public today.)

While Firestone often motored here from the East Coast where he wintered and while he and Edison were close friends, the two men do not seem to be have a bond as strong as that linking Ford and Edison.

Nonetheless the three had a joint project that had resulted from events of World War I. Strategists, scientists and statesmen alike were convinced that one reason Germany lost the war was that it failed to find a source of synthetic rubber when military blockades prevented the import of natural rubber. This was the first war in which rubber had played a major role because it was the first war after the invention of the automobile. Lack of tires meant it was impossible to transport both men and supplies quickly.

In the years following the war, Edison, perhaps encouraged by Firestone, grew very concerned about America's dependence on natural rubber imported from the Far East. He's quoted as saying to Ford, "If war comes, and mark my words it will come, rubber will be the first supply cut off." As a result of his concern, Edison launched a search for a plant that would provide natural rubber, a plant that could be grown in this country.

Obviously, Ford and Firestone had a great deal to gain from this research and both made important contributions. As Robert Halgrim, curator of the Edison Home, explained in an interview, "Ford plowed a lot of money into the Edison Botanical Research lab, which was incorporated in 1928, and Firestone provided lab technicians and research personnel in addition to lab equipment and chemicals needed in the research."

Another ally was then-Secretary of Commerce Herbert Hoover, who procured an appropriation from Congress for purposes of locating sources and encouraging Latin America and the Philippines to produce natural rubber.

Firestone worked with the Liberian government and established a rubber plantation program there. Ford obtained land in Brazil where, after several false starts, he was successful in creating a productive rubber plantation on the Tapajos River.

However, Edison was determined to find a plant that could be grown in this country so we would be independent of even South America and from 1927 until his death in 1931, this project was foremost in his efforts.

According to a Crops Research Report published in July of 1967 by the Agricultural Research Service of the U.S. Department of Agriculture, Edison collected and tested thousands of plants. His research was important to Fort Myers because it was conducted here. The papers were full of it and it was also one of the main reasons President Hoover visited Edison here on his birthday in 1928. In the January 13 edition of its home edition, the *Fort Myers Press* reported on Edison's arrival.

> *It has been Mr. Edison's practice in the past to rest while spending the winter at Seminole Lodge. All this will be changed this winter for the Wizard of Menlo Park plans to work night and day with a corps of highly trained chemists and botanists on the problem of discovering a suitable substitute for the more tropic rubber tree.*

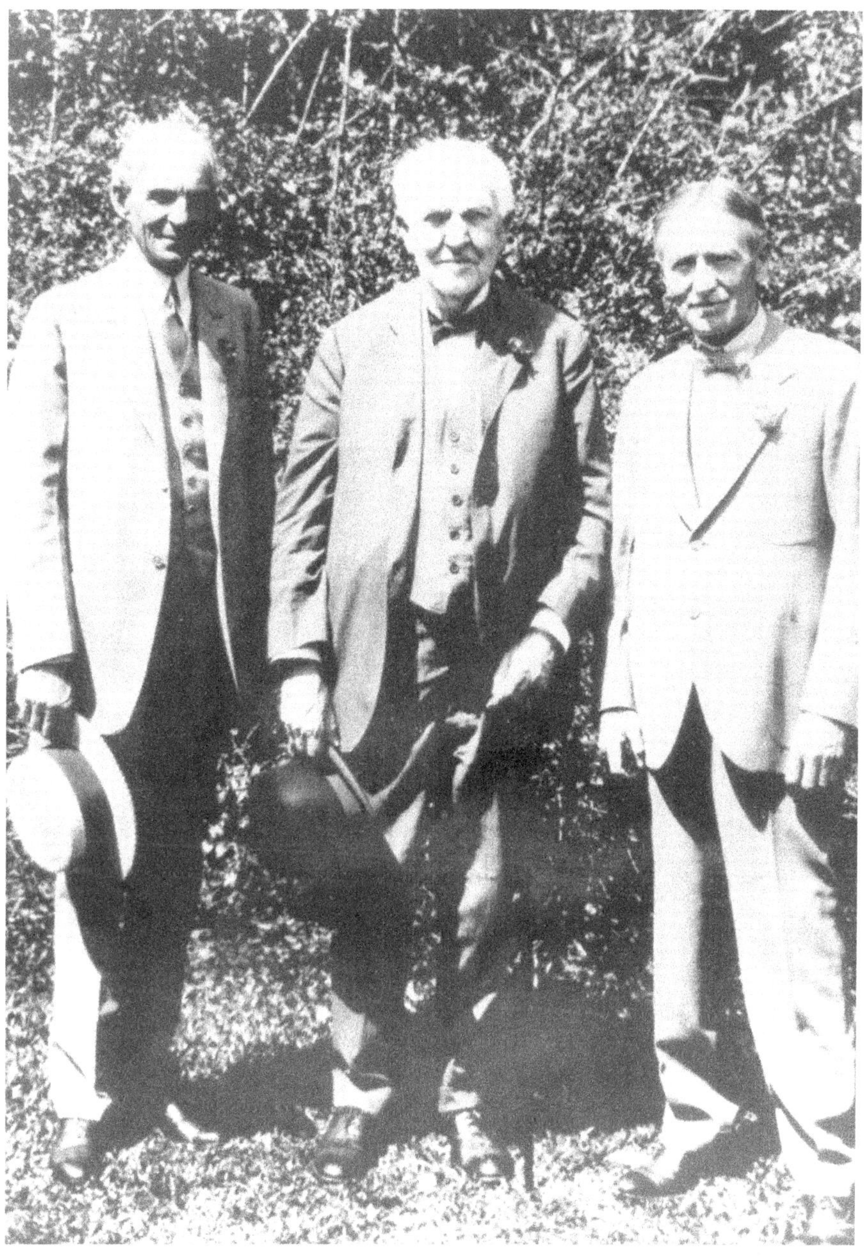

The awesome threesome—Henry Ford, Thomas Edison and naturalist John Burroughs—posed for this photo taken on the grounds of Seminole Lodge. *Courtesy of Southwest Florida Historical Museum.*

This was to be, however, the last winter Edison would work in his original laboratory here. The next year Ford moved the original laboratory and even the ground on which it stood to Greenfield Village in Dearborn, Michigan.

As long-time *News-Press* reporter Robert K. Pepper wrote in a brochure published by the Edison Home, "this city can claim priority to only one of the great inventor's major experiments. And that is the development of natural rubber from the goldenrod weed."

An interesting story is told of Henry Ford in Florence Fritz's book *Bamboo and Sailing Ships*, in which she tells of tourists passing Ford's home on McGregor Boulevard. Not recognizing Ford, who was standing on the sidewalk, they asked if he knew how to get in there. Ford said, "No," and entered the grounds. Shortly afterward, Ford and his wife, Clara, bought the old Everett Hotel at LaBelle and all of old Fort Thompson.

Fritz writes, "The Everett was a rambling wooden structure reached by river steamer. Though it had only two baths—one for 'ladies' and one for 'gents'—to accommodate the 22 high-ceilinged rooms, it had a huge old-fashioned dining room which served delicious meals, frontier style. And lanky Henry Ford and aging Tom Edison enjoyed the lazy river in front and big hatted cowboys and cattle on the dusty road at the back."

Ford, Edison, Firestone and naturalist John Burroughs became famous for the "camping" trips they took each year. Dahlinger writes that the four were not really roughing it because "they were followed by a chuck wagon-type truck, filled with steaks...But they would cook the steaks over a fire they made themselves."

Just prior to his visit in February of 1914, Ford contacted the local Ford dealer and instructed him to have three Model Ts ready for delivery on his arrival. One was for himself; the others were for Edison and Burroughs. When Ford and Burroughs arrived, they were met by a crowd of several thousand people and were escorted to the Edison home by a parade of thirty-one automobiles—every automobile in town at the time.

Pepper shared a delightful anecdote about those Model Ts.

> *The wide gauge wheels fitted the ruts of the old wagon trails in the area—and Edison found the open vehicle quite handy in spitting out tobacco juice. From time to time Ford sent him new parts, and in 1925 a "modern" motor was installed, complete with a self starter. The last change was made in 1927 when the rims were changed to fit a set of goldenrod tires manufactured by Edison's friend, Harvey Firestone...*

> *Edison's practical turn of mind was evidenced by his addiction to the old 1907 Model T Ford touring car...although he was continually urged to take something more modern. But he found the wide gauge of the old chassis handy for following the wagon trails which served for country roads in the early days here...*
>
> *In 1925, when Ford insisted that Edison accept a new Lincoln, he declined saying the old Ford was the most convenient car he had ever seen.*

Pepper concludes by quoting Robert Halgrim, who said,

> *When Mr. Ford pressed Mr. Edison for the reason for the statement, Mr. Edison just chuckled, turned his head and spit some tobacco juice out the side of his mouth. There were no further arguments, and he continued to use the old Ford.*

From the standpoint of local involvement with the automobile, Karl Grismer in *The Story of Fort Myers* shares the intelligence that one of the first cars to arrive in Fort Myers was "a high-wheeled Oldsmobile 'devil-wagon'" driven into town by Dr. Albert Newman. In the meantime, a local man, Ben King, had proven so proficient with automobiles that, according to local history buff Carroll Wadlow, he opened the area's first garage with Archibald English in East Fort Myers near where the railroad intersects Palm Beach Boulevard.

By 1928, the automobile industry had grown to sufficient importance that the *Fort Myers Press* had an automobile page each week during the winter. That same year a gas price war broke out in town. The six Pan Am Stations dropped the price of gasoline by two cents, to twenty cents a gallon. At the same time, Wendell N. Hough had the Chevrolet dealership in a new building at 910 Cleveland Avenue. He was selling The Touring Roadster for $495 and The Coach for $585.

When Edison died in 1931, Ford lost interest in the area and sold his home here. Of course, he had never felt the degree of commitment to the area the Edisons had. And goldenrod tires were never deemed commercially viable.

Originally published in "Only Yesterday" in 1985 in the Fort Myers News-Press.

Edison Park
1926

Edison Park, one of Fort Myers's oldest, most prestigious subdivisions, is an important testimony to the pervasive influence that famed inventor Thomas Alva Edison had on this city.

To reach Edison Park, you must travel south on palm-bedecked McGregor Boulevard, one of the city's main thoroughfares, to the entrance of Edison's winter home. Directly across the Boulevard is Edison's laboratory and a few hundred feet farther south is the entrance to Edison Park. The distance is not great measured in yards, but significant in the years of change the area has weathered.

The entrance is marked by the statue of Minerva, a Grecian maiden holding an urn, modeled after the famous gate in Chestnut Hill, an affluent Philadelphia suburb. When James Newton first commissioned the sculptor, Helmut von Zengen, to create the statue, she was nude. Each day, the sculptor labored behind canvas drapings and each night when he finished his day's work, he carefully covered the art-in-progress beneath tarpaulins. Von Zengen was careful to keep the maiden draped so she would be truly unveiled at the opening ceremonies.

One day Newton was summoned to the Edison home because, he was told, Mrs. Edison had an "important matter" to discuss with him. Upon his arrival, he was informed that certain unidentified ladies of the town were distressed because the statue was nude. No one ever learned how the modest ladies had come by this information.

Newton, understanding the townspeople and sympathizing with their concerns, instructed the sculptor to clothe the statue with the toga it

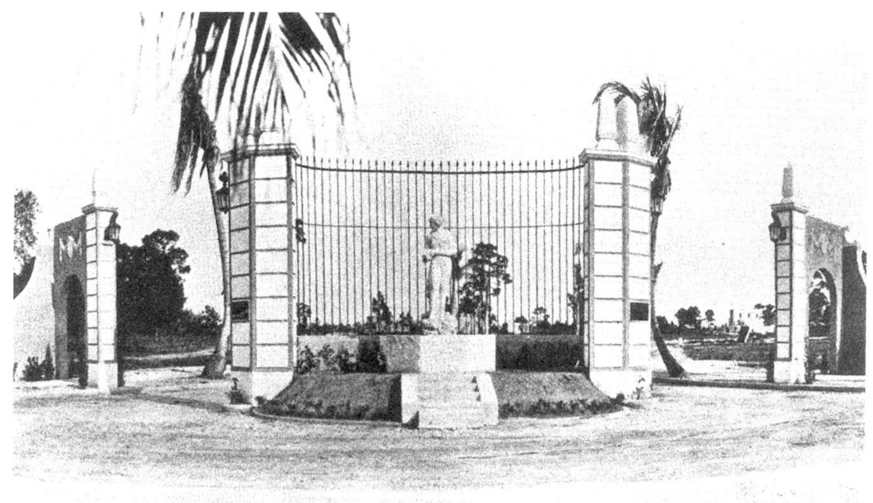

This was the entrance to Edison Park when Jim Newton's subdivision opened in 1926. Note the modestly garbed maiden. Had Mrs. Edison not interceded, the maiden would not have been wearing the gracefully draped toga. *Courtesy of Southwest Florida Historical Museum.*

bears today. He officially unveiled the statue and the subdivision on April 7, 1926.

The opening of the subdivision was an important event. Mina Edison officiated, accompanied by her ailing husband who had risen from his sickbed to attend. Another dignitary on hand was New York State Senator Charles Stadler. Stadler, in addition to being a legislator and millionaire, was active in real estate and developed several subdivisions in Lee County including Stadler's Central Heights, Seminole Park, York Manor Park and Stadler's Farms. The Edisons and Stadler were Newton's friends.

Newton, still active in real estate development in Lee County today, moved to Fort Myers from Philadelphia in 1924 when he was about nineteen. Newton's friendship with Edison began after the two met for the first time while Newton was developing Edison Park, his first business venture in Lee County. Newton recalled recently,

> *Many times I worked right along with the crews and one day I was down in a ditch along McGregor Boulevard shoveling dirt. I'd just dug down and gotten a shovelful and was hefting it up over my shoulder when I looked up and saw Mr. Edison in his Model T Ford looking down*

> *on me. Noting the shovel in my hands, he smiled and from then on, we became good friends. I think he liked people who weren't afraid to spit on their hands and pick up a shovel and do a little hard work.*

Newton still cherishes an inscribed photograph of Edison that reads, "All things come to him who hustles while he waits. To my young friend, Jimmie Newton." It is signed "Thos. A. Edison."

Despite the almost manic quality of the times, for it was the height of the boom in Florida, Newton established a reputation for integrity and excellence. Homes built within Edison Park's fifty-five-acre site were Moorish, Spanish or Italian in design. Lots averaged two-and-a-half acres. Sidewalks were six feet wide. Eight-foot parkways between the curbs and sidewalks were planted with palms, hibiscus, crotons and bougainvillea. Each owner received a written guarantee that the developer would provide curbing, city water and sewers, gas and streetlights.

The local press heaped praise on Newton for his work. One editorial gushed, "Edison Park stands out today as an example to all would-be developers of the past and all developers who may come to this city in the future. It was built by men who kept faith. You developers, old and new, go and do likewise."

Newton did, in fact, decry the puffery and flummery of the era, for in his sales brochure describing Edison Park, he wrote,

> *To the visitor who thinks of Florida as a land of artificiality and real estate booms, the first glimpse of the palm-lined avenues and the homelike character of Fort Myers, the northernmost tropical city in the United States, comes as a distinct surprise. There is none of the feverish excitement, the glitter and bombast one has come to believe is the Florida of today.*

Further on in the brochure. Newton suggested that Florida was a state in transition, and he emphasized a home in Edison Park as an investment in living. The brochure declared,

> *Think what it means to be able to live out of doors all the year 'round—to play golf or tennis or go swimming at Fort Myers Beach every day in the year. Think what it means to see children's eager faces tanned as brown in January as in July, to be able to sit in your patio in the evening, looking up at the Southern Cross in the heaven above, while soft breezes from the Gulf stir the fronds of towering palms…*

Ever the good businessman, Newton did not neglect the financial aspect. "From the viewpoint of investment, Edison Park offers the best opportunity for sound financial profit in the whole state of Florida today," he wrote.

Echoing a problem that is only today being rectified, Newton asserted,

> *For years the development of Fort Myers lagged, because of the handicap of poor roads. Since 1920, when new roads began to be built, the population has increased over 300 percent. To show that this increase represents permanent and not speculative growth, the number of building permits increased 800 percent in the same period. In the first fourteen weeks of 1925, 519 building permits were issued, an increase of 1000 percent in three and one-half months, as compared with the whole twelve months of 1924!*

At the time Edison Park was being developed, Fort Myers was suffering, as reflected in part by the statistics above, and from still another problem which Lee County has only recently alleviated: overcrowded schools. The *Fort Myers Press* reported in January 1924 that "Overcrowded schools are now a big problem. There is one building short and overflow is mostly local. There are 10 to 40 percent more pupils in every building than should be there. Soon it will be tourist season to add to the overcrowding." There are eight buildings now in use.

In September of the following year, double sessions were scheduled at Gwynne Institute—Lee County's first modern school building, constructed in 1911—because of a lack of schoolrooms for the more than two thousand students then registered. According to *The History of Old Lee County Schools*, compiled by historian E.H. "Ned" Loveland, 2,290 school children were enrolled in school during the 1924–25 school year. The following year that number had grown to 3,104!

However, plans involving Edison Park were underway to solve the problem. During 1925, Lee County voters approved an $850,000 bond issue to build two schools: Edison Park Grammar School and another designated simply as "Colored School." By October, local architect I.W. Iredell had completed the plans and specifications, which were advertised in newspapers in Florida, Baltimore and Georgia.

According to the January 1926 minutes of the Lee County Board of Public Instruction, the J.M. Lawton Company won the contract with its bid of $149,500 to build Edison Park Grammar School. Completion was scheduled for August 1. By March, the School Board had settled on property in Edison Park as the site and voted to buy the entire block from Newton's firm, the New Home Development Company, for $68,000.

Newton remembered that transaction. "The School Board didn't have much money so we took school warrants," he remarked. Records indicate the Board paid $26,500 in cash and the balance in $500 installments due at six-month intervals. There were delays in completing the building. In fact, the school didn't open until March 30, 1927; however the cornerstone was laid on March 13, 1926.

The laying of the school cornerstone was an event rivaling the opening of the subdivision in importance. According to an article in the *Fort Myers Tropical News*, all the schools in the city were closed at noon so school children could take part. The Masons of Tropical Lodge 56 were in charge and visiting Masons were instructed to meet at the Elks Club to form a procession of cars to the school site. Music was provided by the Fort Myers Concert Band.

On hand were city Superintendent of Schools Howell L. Watkins and county Superintendent J. Colin English. (English, who has an elementary school named after him on Pine Island Road in North Fort Myers, went on to become state superintendent of schools.) According to Newton, "The Edisons and I were present at the laying of the school cornerstone. In it were placed a photograph of the unveiling of the Edison Park entrance along with a coin." These items (the coin was a dime) were removed in ceremonies commemorating the school's fiftieth anniversary in 1977. Also enclosed were lists of students and faculty. A Cuban Laurel tree donated by Edison was planted on the school grounds that day. That same tree shades today's schoolchildren, as it has flourished over the decades.

In the years that followed, the school became a center of activities not only for its school body and the residents of the subdivision, but also for the community that attended plays and various theatrical offerings in its seven hundred-square foot auditorium, the largest in Lee County at the time. The Lions' Club Minstrels were staged there each year along with little theatre productions, dance recitals by Betty Satchell's students, fish fries, fashion shows and concerts. A recent issue of the *Fort Myers Sun* praised Edison Park for its contribution to civic affairs.

> *It was on the pleasant auditorium of that school that Miss Effie Winkler Henderson McAdow, who taught piano and voice to three generations of the community's children, the late Harry Fagan (president of the First National Bank) and Mrs. George Mann (wife of contractor George Mann and mother of state Representative. Frank Mann)...staged the first events which began the powerful and prestigious Community Concerts.*

The roster of former Edison Park PTA presidents reads like a local who's who. It includes Chesley Perry, president emeritus of the *Fort Myers News-Press*; Frank Watson, attorney for the city of Fort Myers; Circuit Court Judge

Robert Shafer; deceased architect and builder William Frizzell; former County Commissioner Walter Shirey; bank president Chad Wiltshire; advertising executive Dan Harlacher; and local attorney and former member of the Board of Trustees of Edison Community College Travis Gresham, to mention only a few.

Local architect Bill Rivers graduated from Edison Park in 1945. He remembered both the tension of the war years and the flavor and character of life in Fort Myers. The moral code was simple and rigidly enforced. He recalled an incident that took place on the school playground. "I said something like, 'Damn, I don't want to do that,' meaning play softball or something similar and one of the kids heard me. Whoever it was told our sixth grade teacher, Mrs. Redmon, and she took me straight to our principal, Miss Bullock. I had to stay after school in Miss Bullock's office for an entire week."

Sexual permissiveness was a phenomenon of the far distant future, because Rivers also recalled trying to kiss a third grade girl (now a teacher in Lee County) whose name was Jenny Lee Hanshaw. The result? "She slapped me," he reported with a laugh.

Those years were tense, as another incident Rivers recounts demonstrates.

> *Many of the teachers were the wives of pilots stationed at Buckingham Air Force Base in East Fort Myers. I remember one day I heard a rumor the war had ended. This was long before it actually did, but I came back from lunch and told some of the kids. The teachers descended on me and pulled me aside they were so anxious to hear what I had heard.*

Lee County Superintendent of Schools Ray Pottorf was principal of Edison Park School from 1960 through 1964, and he termed those years as "some of my most satisfying professional experiences. It was a close-knit community and extremely supportive of the school," he asserted. "Parents were very involved with their children, the school's activities and the PTA parents were also concerned about their children's educations."

Some of that cooperation was demonstrated when Edison Park teachers, residents and PTA members, along with now-retired School Superintendent Ray L. Williams and then-Deputy School Superintendent Pottorf, built a block-long sidewalk which runs along Edison Avenue. It took three years to raise the money for construction materials and then they built it themselves.

Former third grade teacher Mattie Belle (Mrs. Charles) Gibson also shared fond memories of the school. She taught there from 1929 until

1963, with the exception of eight years leave she took to raise her child. "Fort Myers was small and Edison Park was a new school and, of course, it was a very good neighborhood. Many of the privileged children went there," she reminisced. "Many of the young people attending Edison Park have remained here and have their careers here."

She praised Miss Pearl Bullock, now deceased, who was the principal from the school's opening in 1927 until her retirement in 1959. "Miss Bullock was the very best principal," Mrs. Gibson noted. "She knew the background of every student, the parents, even the grandparents, and she ran the school well." (Miss Bullock was herself a product of Lee County Schools, graduating from the Fort Myers High School class of 1915.)

One of Mrs. Gibson's most vivid memories and favorite stories centers on Doug Grace, a local attorney who today lives on Marlyn Avenue in Edison Park. "Doug Grace," she recalled in an amused voice, "was one of my third graders. And one day he got caught in his seat and we had to call the janitor to free him. Poor Doug was very upset because he thought the janitor was going to have to saw off his arm to free him and nothing we could say would reassure him." The Halgrim family—including Robert C. Halgrim, who for years was curator of the Edison winter home and also received his diploma from Edison on the school's stage—are among the Edison Park alumni. Today Halgrim's son, Robert P. Halgrim, has taken over as curator of the Edison home. Another son, Tommy, is principal of Harlem Heights Elementary School in Lee County.

Edison Park has lived up to developer Jim Newton's sales slogan, "Built To Endure," but in enduring it has changed. It remains a desirable neighborhood, but it is no longer populated entirely by long-time residents. This is reflected in the school as well, for the principal no longer knows each pupil and his or her background.

Nonetheless, even today this historic subdivision with its fine school, its winding, neatly landscaped streets and gracious homes dozes in the sun expressing, as Newton once put it, "none of the feverish excitement, the glitter and bombast one has come to believe is the Florida of today."

And the graceful maiden with the urn stands as a symbol of what Edison Park was—and is.

UPDATE: James D. Newton died December 13, 1990. Robert P. Halgrim died May 5, 2005. Thomas Halgrim died May 22, 2005.

Originally published in the Fall/Winter 1981 edition of Tampa Bay History.

Edison Bridge 1931

Today, the Edison Bridge is overshadowed by the multi-lane Caloosahatchee Bridge, which is west of Lofton's Island. In its day, however, the Edison Bridge was a modern marvel, not only because of its engineering and design, but also because its construction provided jobs for many southwest Floridians during the Great Depression. Its dedication was also one of the most important events in the fledgling city's history.

As early as October 1930, the people living in the East End of Fort Myers were concerned about the impact that the new Edison Bridge would have on their businesses; so concerned, in fact, that five hundred signed a petition asking that the wooden bridge at the end of Fremont Street be kept open. They reasoned that traffic would continue to grow, and there would be a need for an additional bridge because of "narrow and dangerous bottlenecks at Weaver's Corner (where Old 41 and Bayshore Road/Pine Island Road intersect) and at First and Fowler on either side of the Edison Bridge," according to the residents' petition, printed in the *Fort Myers Tropical News*.

The East Enders were also concerned that the closing would reduce the value of their property and cause a decrease in business because a substantial "part of the patronage of the merchants in that section is derived from residents living north of the river," the paper reported. The Fremont Bridge was several miles east of the Edison Bridge.

Their concern was justified not only because development and business had already slowed in east Fort Myers, but also by the fact that the nation was in the throes of the Great Depression. Each issue of the *Tropical News* carried stories about banks closing and the high unemployment rate.

Harry Stringfellow, then chairman of the board of county commissioners, delayed the closing of the wooden bridge, commenting that the cost of maintaining the span would be only seventy-five dollars a month.

By the end of 1930, the new bridge was almost complete and plans for the dedication were being formed. At first it was thought that officials would schedule the dedication on January 14, 1931, to coincide with the visit of one hundred fliers and forty planes that would be stopping at the municipal airport, but that plan was shelved.

Instead, a committee headed by Fort Myers mayor Josiah Finch, Sheriff F.B. Tippins, Carl R. Roberts and Dave Ireland decided the dedication should fall on Thomas Alva Edison's eighty-fourth birthday, which was on February 11.

For a month prior to the dedication excitement built in Fort Myers, beginning with the Edisons' return to their winter home, Seminole Lodge. On January 16, 1931, the *Tropical News* announced in bold headlines, "Edisons to start to Fort Myers Next Tuesday."

The article was filled with tidbits of information. "The Edisons…with their son and daughter-in-law, Mr. and Mrs. Charles Edison, and a number of friends will entertain at Newark, N.J. at 9:30 a.m., and will probably arrive in Fort Myers Wednesday evening."

The article went on to say that six of Edison's assistants were scheduled to arrive that day with the equipment Edison would need to continue his rubber experiments. Fred Ott, his veteran right-hand man, was to be among them and the *Tropical News* shared the tidbit that "to Mr. Ott annually falls the duty of shining up the brass radiator of the inventor's 1914 model T Ford and having it at the station when they arrive."

Wednesday's paper on January 21 included the front-page news that the Edisons were on their way south along with the Harvey Firestones and James D. Newton, now a realtor and developer, but then an assistant to Firestone.

The article described Edison as "weary" and said interviewers had quoted him as saying the first thing he wanted to do when he was arrived was rest. This should have provided a clue to the people of Fort Myers of what was to happen, but it didn't.

The Edisons' arrival time in Fort Myers was uncertain, "but whatever time they come in," the *Tropical News* reported, "they will get a reception at the station—not a formal reception with a silk-hatted welcoming committee,

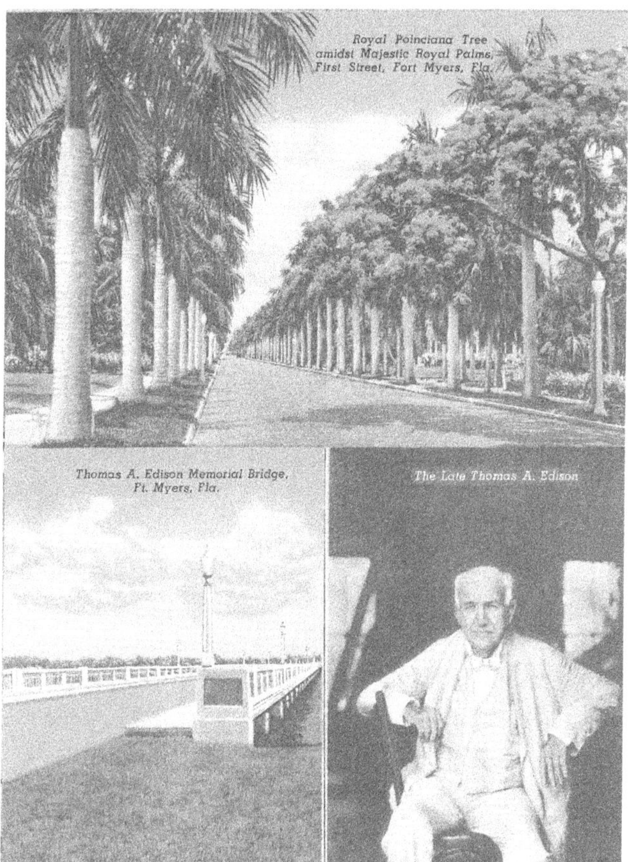

The Edison Bridge was dedicated on Edison's birthday, February 11, 1931. *Courtesy of Southwest Florida Historical Museum.*

keys to the city, and a brass band—but hearty greetings from scores of old friends who have bidden them welcome for most of the 48 years they have been coming here."

Some of the plans formulated for the dedication at this point included having Edison press an electrically wired button that would close the draw span. Then the officials would drive across the bridge with Ford in the 1914 car, which would be preceded by an oxcart, if one could be found, followed by the modern cars of the spectators.

Nat G. Walker, the architect who designed the post office (now the Judge George W. Whitehurst Federal Building) was appointed chairman of the dedication committee.

The next day, banner headlines announced "Edisons Home Here For 48th Winter." In a smaller headline, it was reported that they had "Come in a Special Car as Friends Wait at Wrong Depot."

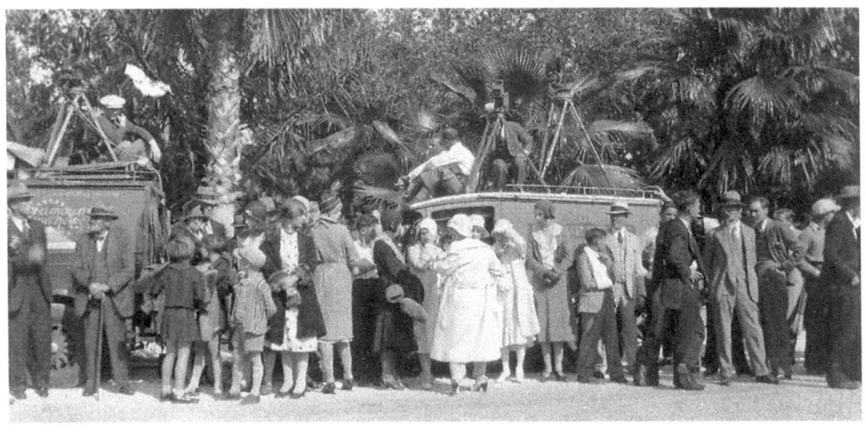

The dedication of the Edison Bridge brought out the national media and then, as now, photographers waited atop trucks so they could get the best angles. *Courtesy of Southwest Florida Historical Museum.*

> *While friends waited to greet them at the Atlantic Coast Line station, Mr. and Mrs. Edison slipped into Fort Myers unobserved on a Seaboard Air Line special train and were settled down for their 48th annual winter sojourn at Seminole Lodge before anybody was aware of their arrival.*

However, Fort Myers residents did not resent the deception, and the next day they read in the *Tropical News* that, "For the first time in the memory of any members of his staff, Thomas Alva Edison failed to visit his laboratory on the first day after arrival." Edison's health was failing. Indeed, he was to die on October 12 of that year, and his participation in the dedication of the bridge was reduced to a minimum.

This is not to say that the dedication itself was to be in any way reduced. Now it was announced that "a bevy of about 20 girls dressed in white in automobiles would escort Mr. Edison to the Trail Fountain [which used to be roughly where the Caloosahatchee Bridge's overpass is today], where the rest of the parade would fall in line."

The Tamiami Trail Blazers—a group described by Karl Grismer as "a small band of good road boosters" who drove from Fort Myers to Miami (the trip took three weeks) to point out the need for the Everglades portion of the Tamiami Trail—were to form one of the units. And there were to be three bands: the Fort Myers Concert Band, the junior band and the American Legion Drum & Bugle Corps, which would form a guard of honor.

At this point, plans also called for an evening dance to be held on the bridge after the dedication. "Although the surface is quite rough, the committee thought it could be made suitable for dancing by the application of corn meal," according to the *Tropical News*.

Times were so difficult that Mayor Fitch had announced a couple of days earlier that a free employment agency was to be set up in City Hall. So the estimate of $200 as the cost of the ceremonies was quite a bit of money. Stringfellow said he'd ask county commissioners to approve the money and Mayor Fitch said the city would pick up any expenses over the $200.

The news coverage in the days that followed was very revealing. On the one hand, it demonstrated that the Edisons did not merely spend their winters here, but were active in the community. It also pointed up the respect and affection with which the community regarded them as well as their power.

In a short item on the society pages, society editor Margaret Mickle reported January 29 that Mina Edison had attended a meeting of the Valinda Literary Society and had encouraged the Society to support the American Red Cross, which was massing a drive to raise ten million dollars to help drought-stricken farmers in Arkansas and throughout the Midwest.

The local Red Cross chapter had voted not to participate but by the following day, the item had reached the front page. Headlines read, "Mrs. Edison Urges Red Cross Drive Board to Consider." It did and Fort Myers worked to ante up its share: $1,400.

This was followed by a report of a visit to town by Mr. and Mrs. Edison. At the time, a "highway locomotive sound wagon" was positioned on First Street advertising Majestic radios. W.P. Franklin was the Majestic dealer and Mrs. Edison had approached Franklin and H.O. McGee, who was operating the wagon, and asked to use the equipment to launch the Red Cross drive. Both agreed.

Then she suggested that oranges be sold to raise money for the Red Cross, whereupon Franklin sent home for the oranges he had there. These were sold to bystanders for five to fifty cents.

Before the Edisons returned home, Franklin had collected about fifty dollars. For this he was to purchase additional oranges, pay for their transportation to the Edisons' friends up north and the proceeds were to go to the Red Cross. The paper never indicated that either McGee or Franklin were members of the Red Cross, but it is certain that they completed their assigned tasks.

Edison, who had waited in the car all this while, was quoted as saying, "I'm sick of the whole radio business and I guess you fellows are pretty sick of it, too."

Mrs. Edison was also responsible for having girls man tables in hotel lobbies during the dedication ceremonies so that people wishing to make contributions to the Red Cross might do so.

Still another example of her role in the community took place the same week, when the *Fort Myers Tropical News* sponsored its fourth free cooking school. Mrs. Edison shared the platform on opening day with Mayor Fitch and her remarks posed the question, "Do not the rosy cheeks of our children and the smile of happy approval of our husbands compensate the mother for all the time it takes to prepare a tempting dish?" She took issue with women who depended too heavily on canned foods, saying, "We are neglecting our tables and meals are made up of canned articles, which are ushered into our stomachs at the rate of automobile and airplane speed." An editorial the next day praised Mrs. Edison for her expertise.

As the time before the dedication grew shorter, the paper dutifully reported when she spoke to the Periwinkle Garden Club and when she took a group of friends to dinner at the Gondola Inn, which was on the river off West First Street, west of where M.F. Hagan's Seafood Packers is now.

Next it was reported that the celebration would start at 2:30 p.m. when twenty-four girls would accompany the Edisons to First and Carson Streets. Two eighteen-by-thirty-inch bronze plaques costing $130 would be unveiled at the bridge and a band of Seminole Indians brought by W. Stanley Hanson, their "white medicine man for 20 years," would participate in the parade.

Plans for the dedication now also included the Egypt Shrine band from Tampa because Estes B. Fletcher, the Imperial Shrine potentate, would unveil and dedicate the plaques.

Robert Bentley, chairman of the state road department, announced that he was postponing the department's annual budget meeting one week so that he could attend. An oxcart had been found in Buckingham and Governor Doyle E. Carlton had agreed to attend and speak.

In addition, Ruth Parker, who had delivered telegrams to Edison when he had first visited fifty years earlier (at that time, her mother, Laura Thompson, had been the telegraph operator) was to ride a white horse in the parade. The Henry Fords had not yet arrived and so for the first time in four years would not be on hand to help Edison celebrate his birthday. But Harvey Firestone was, and Cyrus H.K, Curtis, publisher of *Saturday Evening Post Magazine* and described by the *Tropical News* as "a new friend," had motored over from Miami to be with Edison.

The day finally arrived. The *Tropical News* described First Street as "flag bedecked," thanks probably in no small part to Colonel H.A. Dixon, who had the title of city flag sergeant.

W.B. Seabrooks of the merchants association announced that stores and businesses would remain open and schoolchildren were let out early and marched in a line to the corner of Fowler Street, where a temporary platform had been erected.

The next day the *Tropical News* reported that ten thousand people thronged the area while Edison "untied a big bow knot in an orange and green ribbon, gave a whoop and waved his hands above his head and the new concrete span was officially dedicated."

Bentley reported that the Edison Bridge, which was 8,100 feet long and cost $667,159 to build, was one of three which would modernize traffic to Fort Myers; the others were in Bradenton and Punta Gorda. Bentley also announced that work on the final link of the road from Fort Myers to West Palm Beach would commence in the Fall.

Governor Carlton—sporting a scar alongside his left eye and a bandaged right hand, both the result of a recent accident—promised that he would recommend to the legislature that the state real estate tax be repealed.

Perhaps the shocker of the day was that, as the *Tropical News* reported, "For the first time in the history of Edison's birthday celebrations, several person[s]reported to the police that their pockets had been picked while they watched the exercises."

Police Chief W.A. Wells and Deputy Sheriff Jerry Collins apprehended the two out-of-town men for the thefts, which had amounted to $120.

And in the same paper it was reported that the U.S. Senate had voted to buy two thousand square miles in the Everglades for Everglades National Park (which would open in 1947 in ceremonies officiated at by President Harry S. Truman), and that Edison was now "consuming only milk," his birthday cake—which Queenie, the cook at the Seminole Lodge, had baked, using fresh coconut—was being auctioned slice by slice at the Heitman Arcade to raise money for the Red Cross.

In his remarks, Mayor Fitch spoke for Fort Myers when he said, "Today we are touching a high spot in the history of Fort Myers. Whatever efforts we make to honor Mr. Edison will fall short of his honor to us."

UPDATE: The Edison Bridge has since been torn down.

Originally published in the July 22, 1984 edition of the Fort Myers News-Press.

The Edison Pageant 1938

Curvaceous coeds in their brief bikinis wave down at the crowds from the gaily-colored floats. Drum majors lift high their batons for the downbeat that fills the air with the clang of cymbals and the roll of drums. Silver foil dolphins and papier-mâché palm trees sway with the movement of their motorized carriers as do the mock thrones, on which are seated kings and queens, princes and princesses. Yes, it's Edison Pageant time! The streets and avenues of Fort Myers come alive with visitors. Store windows are vibrant with the beauty of tropical blossoms and boughs twisted into intricate designs and arrangements. First Street is lined with chairs as parade enthusiasts stake their claims to the curbside from which they are guaranteed a front row seat for the parade.

If, however, you think the Edison Pageant of Light is the only pageant Fort Myers has ever hosted, you're in the majority, but you're wrong. Fort Myers's love affair with parades, street dances, coronations—with pageants, goes back a long way, in fact to the very early years of the twentieth century.

The first pageant was called "Conquesta de Florida," and it lasted four days. The first three days, the Spaniards, portrayed by the adults in the community, would try to invade Fort Myers. The invaders would travel up the river in boats owned by local fishing guides and attempt to land near the site of today's Ramada Inn. During a fiercely play-acted battle, they would be driven back by the Indians, acted by the young people. On the third day, the Spaniards would succeed and pretend to burn the Indians at the stake in ceremonies at League Park, which stood on what is today the Boulevard Plaza. The fourth day was the festival's highlight. Large bags of cornmeal would be spread on the asphalt brick pavement of First Street for the street dance, but before that came the big event: the parade. The floats were primitive compared to the $40,000 and $50,000 beauties in today's parades, but the early crowds received them with enthusiasm matching our own today. Marchers dressed as Spanish conquistadores or Indians, although some genuine Seminoles traveled up from the Everglades to lend a note of authenticity to the occasion.

Picture in your mind's eye, the ladies standing alongside First Street, melting from the heat of the blazing noon sun within their high-necked, full length dresses. Imagine the clumsiness of their movements as they traveled about encased in stiff metal corsets and bustles and further encumbered by the parasols they carried to protect their skin. Envision mischievous little boys wearing knickers and blousy shirts with collars and long, full sleeves darting through the crowd, pushing through to the curb so they could see. And the schoolgirls wearing high-topped button shoes, long skirts and blouses with ties as they stood demurely, eyes almost lowered, to watch the parade.

Fort Myers had sidewalks made of wooden planking then and no gutters. The only paved section was that block of First Street that today runs between Jackson and Hendry Streets. Elsewhere in town, ditches ran alongside the hard-packed clay streets and the remnants of the quick afternoon showers stood in puddles.

There were other differences, contrasts more significant than the construction of the streets. The pace of day-to-day living was much slower. Life wasn't as abundant, as filled with "things" as it is today, but people had time to stop and talk with and help one another. And people were much thriftier; in fact, thrift was one of the most respected virtues. This was amply demonstrated in the early parades; they used what they had to make the floats, including palmetto fronds, Spanish moss and red, white and blue bunting left over from the last Fourth of July picnic. Horses, Model Ts and Model As provided transportation.

But most importantly, Conquesta de Florida was a celebration of America and American values. One of the signs read "A Nation In The Making" and the flags of America, Spain and France were among those carried, but the biggest was "Old Glory" and cheers rang out as she passed.

This, then, was Fort Myers's first known pageant, but it was far from her last. However, while the Conquesta de Florida was never officially disbanded, as the years passed and World War I broke out, interest waned.

The foundation for the next pageant was laid during the real estate boom in 1928. Fort Myers was awash with developers, promoters and money. More significantly, while pageants were far from anyone's mind, promotion and publicity weren't.

At the time, Jimmy Crafton, then secretary of the Chamber of Commerce, came up with the idea of a pageant celebrating one of Fort Myers's most popular assets: the abundant sunshine. The newly created Sunshine Court he instigated celebrated one thousand days of continuous sunshine—days when the sun, even if it didn't shine brightly, was at least seen even if briefly. In 1937, the year he moved to St. Petersburg, Crafton was Sunshine King, a title he passed to Ronald Halgrim. In St. Petersburg, Crafton started a similar Sun Festival. The *St. Petersburg Times* even gave away newspapers on days when the sun failed to shine.

Ronald Halgrim was city editor of the *Fort Myers News-Press*. As a reporter he was well known to Edison because he had interviewed Edison many times, along with the celebrities who visited the inventor. In later years, Ronald Halgrim wrote these words about Edison's birthday for a pageant program, "Among those who usually celebrated his birthday with the inventor were Henry Ford, Harvey Firestone, Herbert Hoover, Dan Beard, and some of the Edison pioneers." (Beard was an American artist and writer, best known as one of the founders of the Boy Scouts of America.) The Edison Pioneers were men who had worked with Edison for twenty-five years before he died. The group still exists today, but now it consists of anyone who worked for Edison for any length of time.

Edison's birthday on February 11 had become a national event and brought many famous people to Fort Myers who claimed friendship with the "living immortal." The birthday was also the occasion for an annual interview in which Edison would answer all questions. The writers and reporters would work for days on a list of approximately forty questions covering everything from his inventions to his opinion on our nation's politics to world affairs.

All of Fort Myers was saddened by Edison's death in 1931. The following year, 1932, memorial services were held on his birthday and in the years 1935, 1936 and 1937 church services conducted by ministers from all denominations were held throughout the small community. And the community was small. According to the U.S. Census, Lee County had a population of 14,990 in 1930.

When Ronald Halgrim stepped to the helm of the Sunshine Pageant in 1938, he had already been active in the memorial services for Edison for some time. He felt the Sunshine Pageant might be a vehicle suitable to express his and the community's respect and appreciation as well as affection for Thomas Edison. Thus, the first Edison Pageant of Light was celebrated in February 1938.

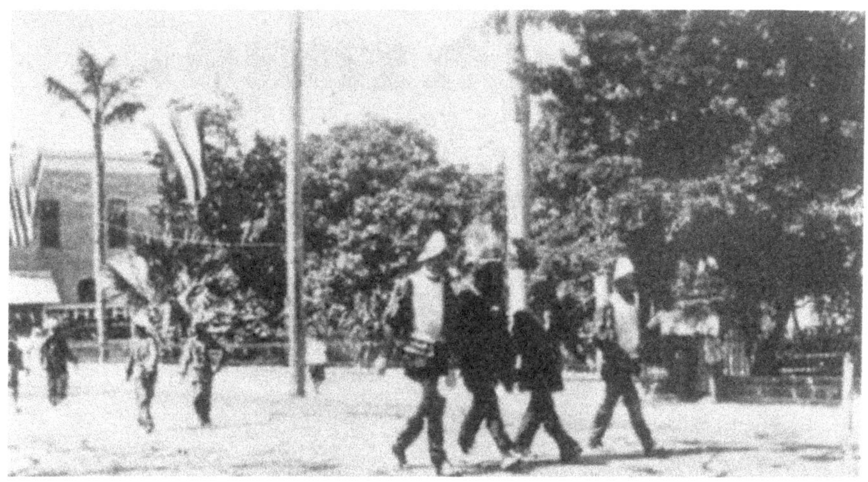

These marchers were participating in Conquesta de Florida, Fort Myers's first pageant, the precursor to the Edison pageant. *Courtesy of Southwest Florida Historical Society.*

Halgrim received support and help with that first pageant from the Women's Community Club and the Jaycees. It lasted three days and featured a coronation ball for the members of the newly formed Court of Edisonia, which supplanted the Sunshine Court. The ball was held at the Town Club, which is still in use but now owned and operated by the Rabe O. Wilkinson American Legion Post No. 38. The building, which was built by the Elks Lodge 1288, is situated on First Street near the intersection of Evans Avenue. According to the pageant program of 1969, the royal robes and jewels for that first pageant were shipped by air express from Philadelphia for the coronation. Homer Mercer's Orchestra drove down from Tampa to play for the ball.

At the first coronation Ronald Halgrim passed the royal scepter on to the new and very first king and queen of Edisonia—James Hendry III and Virginia Sheppard Holloway. Sidney Davis, as the royal lord chamberlain, crowned the new royalty before four hundred ballgoers who applauded as the royal couple ascended to their palmetto-bedecked thrones.

At that time, Fort Myers Mayor David Shapard was operating the Bradford Hotel on First Street. It was in his capacity as mayor, however, that he addressed the group, expressing the feelings of most Fort Myers residents when he said, "Mankind was made better by Thomas Alva Edison having lived and Fort Myers was made a better place to live."

The pageant was held during the next years until February of 1942. By that time, our nation was in the throes of World War II and the pageant was not celebrated again until 1946. In the meantime, pageant founder Ronald Halgrim died in August 1945.

In its early years, the coronation ceremony and ball were held at the Municipal Pier. Now long gone, the pier was on what is now the site of the new Caloosahatchee Bridge. These rites were also held in the Arcade Theatre, the Civic Center (now part of the Chamber of Commerce on Edwards Drive), the auditorium of Fort Myers High School and even in a circus tent rented from Ringling Brothers Circus, then wintering in Sarasota.

One of the most colorful and significant ceremonies was the 1946 coronation ball, which was held in a hangar at Buckingham Air Force Field. This event had a special meaning for Robert Halgrim, Ronald's brother, who had worked for Edison. "Mrs. Edison was there and Charles Edison too," he recalls. "She asked me that year if I would be curator of Edison's Fort Myers home and laboratory if she gave it to the city. I told her I would."

Both were as good as their word. The Edison home was opened to the public in November of 1947 with Halgrim as curator and Fred Lowdermilk, formerly city superintendent of public works, as manager. Halgrim served in that capacity until 1973 when he retired. Now his son, Robert C. Halgrim, is curator.

A great many events have been added to the pageant over the years, including the shell show (1963), the strolling flower show (unique to Fort Myers), the children's parade, the golf, tennis, shuffleboard and card tournaments, the science fair exhibits and boat races.

Over the years, many features of the pageant have become almost traditional, including the Edison Birthday Party, which was started in 1959 by Mrs. George T. Mann. At the birthday party, a huge cake is cut by a member of the Edison family. The Edison Choral Society, a group of local singers who organize each year for this event, presents musical numbers. There are also skits, dance acts and comedy routines all featuring local talent. And refreshments are served to the public—after all, it is a birthday party.

According to an article in the 1963 pageant program by local newspaperwoman Joyce Turner Black that parade, which was the first held in the daytime, drew twelve thousand spectators. It was composed of forty decorated floats and cars, four bands, a bicycle brigade and a marching delegation. The Grand Parade of Light has now become one of the highlights of the pageant and annually draws several hundred thousand viewers. The number of entries exceeds two hundred.

Robert Halgrim summed it up this way. "We have several hundred local people who work each year to put on the Pageant. They sell memberships to finance it and they organize all the events. It's all done locally. The Pageant

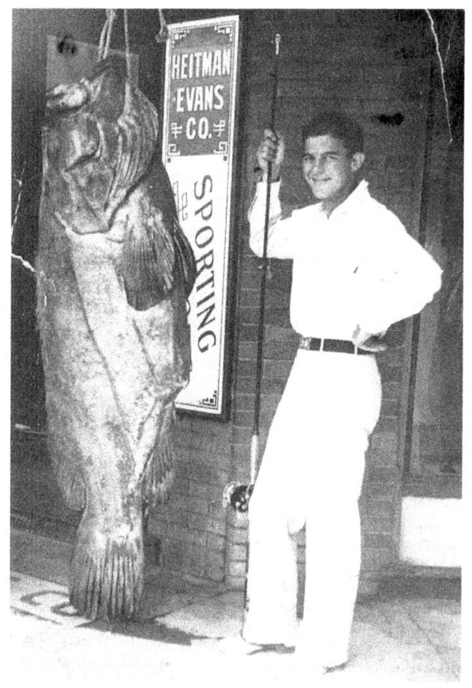

Fort Myers New-Press editor Ronald Halgrim, shown in this photo with a massive fish, is arguably the founder of the Edison Pageant, since it was his idea to change the Sunshine Court into a pageant honoring Thomas Alva Edison. *Courtesy of Southwest Florida Historical Society.*

has given the community the feeling of working together for the good of our town and our people."

In 1914, Thomas Edison said, "There is only one Fort Myers and 90 million people are going to find it out." With those words in mind, Edison today would be not only revered as an inventor, but a prophet as well.

UPDATE: In 1988, demand for more public events was great, but the pageant membership available to provide volunteer leadership for more activities was limited. In a unanimous vote, the board of directors of the pageant elected to turn over public events of the Edison Pageant of Light to a newly-formed, non-profit corporation. Following the 1989 Edison Pageant of Light, the new organization, the Edison Festival of Light, Inc. officially assumed responsibility for all of the pageant's public events.

Originally published in February 1980 in Lee Living.

Willard Lamb Velie: The Other Car Magnate 1920

Although not much is known of the Willard Velie family, Henry Ford was not the only auto manufacturer to winter in Fort Myers. The Velies, manufacturers of a number of models but best known for Old Maud, built a home and wintered here during the 1920s.

Willard Lamb Velie was the third son of Stephen H. Velie Sr. and Emma Deere, daughter of John Deere, which made him John Deere's grandson. He graduated from Yale in 1888 and started his career by working as secretary to the Deere & Company Board of Directors, the world's largest plow manufacturer. Instead of remaining with the family business in Moline, Illinois, Velie did the unexpected. He followed Horace Greeley's admonition to "Go west, young man" and took the first step in a journey that would ultimately lead him to winter in Fort Myers. At the time, however, his destination was the frontier state of Montana. There he married Annie Floweree, his roommate's sister. His bride was also the daughter of Daniel Augustus Greene Floweree, the millionaire cattle rancher from Helena who settled next to the Murphy-Burroughs Home in the winter of 1898.

By 1890, Velie was back in the family fold, working as a clerk in Deere & Co. Within a year, he'd done his penance, served his apprenticeship and was named sales manager. In 1895, following the death of his father, he was elected corporate secretary and a member of the board of directors. He and his wife had two children: Willard Lamb Velie Jr. and Marjorie.

On May 19, 1901, the first automobile came to Moline with Hi Henry's Minstrel Show. It might have influenced Velie somewhat, but whatever the reason, within months he resigned as secretary. In January of 1902, he formed the Velie Carriage Co. to build carriages and wagons.

Following the death of his uncle Charles in 1907, Velie decided he wanted to build cars. After all, it was the future of transportation. On July 2, 1908, the Velie Motor Vehicle Company was incorporated in Illinois and had its first great success that same year when it debuted with a popular, affordable and reliable car called the Velie 30, more familiarly known as Old Maud. The price was $1,750. By 1909, Velie had made and sold his first thousand cars. Four short years later the company had $1.5 million in company assets. In 1920 the company produced nine thousand cars.

For the first six years, the Velie motorcars were advertised in John Deere Plow Company catalogs and listed along with farm equipment. In 1915, Velie decided the car would do better if it was demonstrated in an auto showroom and sold by dealers.

In 1911, Velie also began manufacturing trucks and by 1915, the salesman's manual listed 360 companies that used Velie trucks including Armour & Co., Goodyear and International Harvester. And in 1911, the Velie was defined by the advertising slogan selected to represent the product: "The Climax in Auto Value."

Within the next decade the Velies began wintering in Fort Myers because of ties with the Flowerees. They built a home next to Mrs. Velie's father on the Caloosahatchee where the Sea Chest Motel is today, on First Street between Poinsettia and Woodford.

Jane Gorton Brecht, whose father Al Gorton was at one time a Velie dealer, was too young to remember much except that the Velies gave elegant parties yet kept very much to themselves. Certainly they were never active in the community, never joining organizations or doing charity work as Mrs. Edison had done.

Sara King Rasmussen, who has lived in Tallahassee many years, was a child growing up in Fort Myers during the period the Velies wintered here; however, because of her father, Mrs. Rasmussen remembers more than most people.

> *I remember my father, Ben King—he owned King's Garage on Jackson and had the agency for many of the cars of the time—talking about Marjorie Velie, the daughter. She had a red sports car similar to a MG. She and Daddy struck up a friendship related to fast cars and he loved to drive her little runabout. I don't know when that would have been. Probably about 1919 or 1920.*

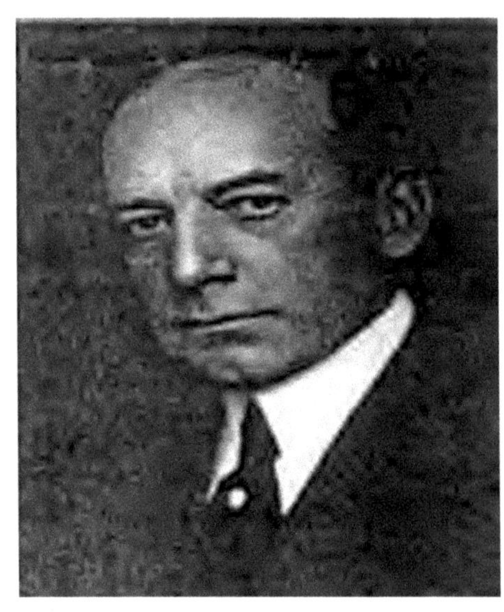

Willard Lamb Velie. *Photo from author's archives.*

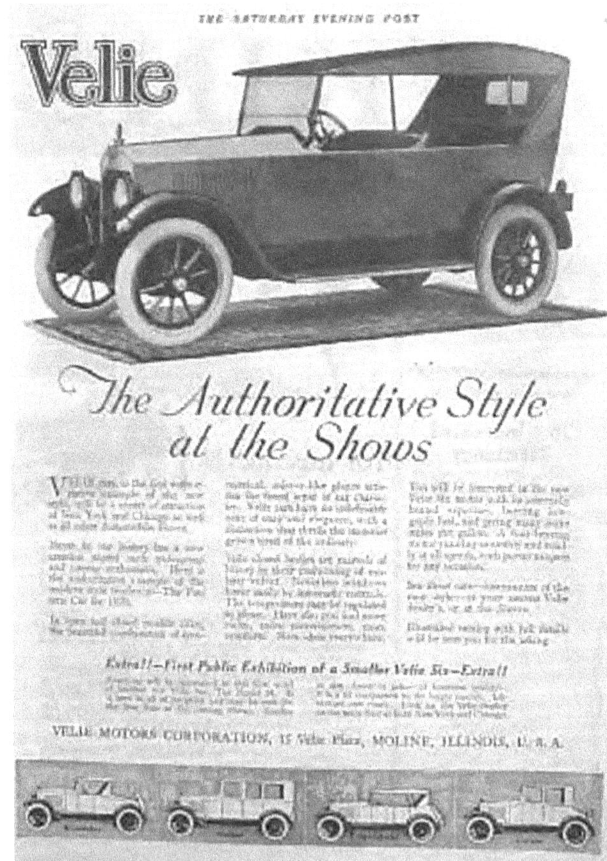

This ad for Velie automobiles appeared in the *Saturday Evening Post* and marked the company's introduction of a new smaller model. *Photo from author's archives.*

Mrs. Rasmussen remembers Marjorie Velie as "a tall, attractive young woman, probably about 20 years old." She also remembers the car. "When I was 12 or 13," she writes, "Daddy owned a Velie among other cars, and it became sort of 'my' car. There were no driver's licenses in those days, and I drove it to school each day. That would be 1924 or 1925. The Gages later bought the Velie property and the Velies were heard from no more."

Actually, the Velies manufactured cars until 1928. They announced the new models for 1929, but never produced them. This failure was not linked to the stock market crash, but to the death of Will Velie who passed away suddenly on October 24, 1928, in Moline. His son closed the factory for the funeral, but announced he would continue the motorcar line. His son, however, was manufacturing aircraft and couldn't handle both. He discontinued production of automobiles in November and died of heart disease on March 20, 1929. The home in Fort Myers was purchased by the John Gage family from Chicago.

Today, the Velie automobile is remembered only by automobile buffs, but in its day it was prized for its combination of quality and low price. In 1922, the United States Naval Department in New York conducted intense and demanding tests of seventy-six foreign and domestic passenger cars. The purpose of the tests was to select the best features of automobile motors and engineers for adaptation to aircraft. Only eight passed the tests. The eight were the Dusenberg, the Fiat, the Packard, the Brewster, the Hispana Suiza, the Marmon, the Issota Franchina and the Velie.

Originally published in "Only Yesterday" in 1984 in the Fort Myers News-Press.

Thomas Goolsby: The Death of a Boy Scout 1928

This month marks the seventy-fifth anniversary of the founding of the Boy Scouts of America. The Boy Scouts were and are an important segment in the lives of youngsters in Fort Myers. Until recent years, when the area has grown so large, Boy Scout activities were reported in the newspaper and residents turned out en masse when the Scouts had their jamborees and camporamas. The fate of one young scout touched residents here so deeply that he is still remembered and was honored at ceremonies held this week by Boy Scout Troop No. 1.

The scout was Thomas Goolsby, sixteen, the son of Charles and Sarah Goolsby. It was summertime in Fort Myers. Goolsby was working at a summer job as usher at the Arcade Theatre on First Street. He was well known in town. Of course, Fort Myers was a small community, but young Goolsby had made a mark for himself the previous January when he'd been a member of a party of one hundred Boy Scouts who had visited Cuba. The *Tropical News* had written, "In Fort Myers his proud parents listened in over the radio as their boy received the highest honors of the scout world, an eagle badge, presented by President Machado of Cuba."

The tragedy began Saturday July 7, 1928, when Goolsby fell ill, so ill that he didn't report to work at the Arcade. His sister, Mrs. Marjorie (W.W.) Stewart remembers it as being a difficult time for their mother and for their father, a builder who was constructing a home in Canal Point.

The *Tropical News* reported, "The family physician, Dr. George S. Stone, was summoned and said he believed Thomas was suffering from an attack of ptomaine poisoning. By yesterday (Tuesday), he had apparently recovered, but early in the afternoon the boy became critically ill and passed away shortly afterwards."

The death of a child is always a shock, but the loss was felt even more keenly in Fort Myers because the residents were close. This was reflected in the next paragraph of the article, which continued, "Thomas was being mourned last night by a grief-stricken mother, his father who was hurrying home from Canal Point and a wide circle of friends—boys who cherished him as a pal, hundreds of older persons who knew him as an enterprising young businessman, and his scoutmaster and scout executive, R.L. Newman Jr. and H.O. Kight, both of whom described him as 'an ideal boy.'"

The *Fort Myers Press* wrote, "Thomas was loved by a wide circle of friends who honored him for his attainments as an Eagle Scout and the cheery smile with which he greeted all Arcade patrons."

At first, plans were to hold a church funeral, but these were abandoned when it was learned he had died from spinal meningitis. On Friday, it was announced that "brief commitment services would be held at his graveside."

Even in death, the Boy Scouts played a major role in Goolsby's life, for the *Tropical News* reported that Friday—ironically, it was the thirteenth—that Goolsby's Boy Scout comrades would carry his body to its final resting place in the Fort Myers Cemetery. The scouts who assembled at Engelhardt's Funeral Home that sad morning were Henry Colquitt Jr., John Smith, Jack Morris, Robert Morris, Wilbur Wright and Glenn Bryant.

The community's response was immediate. "Less than an hour after 'Taps' had been sounded in the Fort Myers cemetery for Thomas Goolsby," the *Tropical News* reported, "plans were being made at the luncheon of the Civitan Club for the erection of a Boy Scout headquarters in the city hall park as a memorial to the young Eagle Scout."

"Determined to preserve the memory of Thomas Goolsby, Eagle Scout, hailed by H.O. Kight as an example of perfect boyhood," wrote the *Fort Myers Press*.

The Civitans invited all the city's luncheon clubs to join in the project, which was suggested by Harry G. Switzer who was then the manager of the Palm City Brick & Tile Co. It was decided to "construct the building by contributions of material and labor" and Switzer, who put his heart where his mouth was, opened the campaign by offering to furnish material for the building of the walls.

And a great deal of progress had been made even prior to the meeting because tentative plans for a one-story structure about twenty-five by fifty feet in size were discussed. And it was decided that Kight's office would be included in the memorial building along with space for Boy Scout displays.

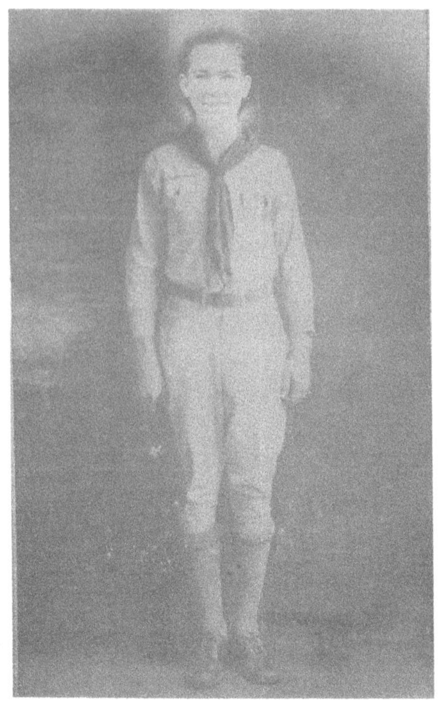

Thomas Goolsby, a Fort Myers Eagle Scout who died at a tragically young age, lived his life so honorably that the entire town grieved when he passed. *Courtesy of Southwest Florida Historical Museum.*

After voting unanimously in favor of adopting the project, the Club stood in silence for one minute in honor of Goolsby and "Short talks on the virtues of the youth were made by James Calderhead, Scoutmaster R.L. Newman Jr. and Jim C. Clements," the *Press* noted.

The Civitans followed through, submitting the plans to the Fort Myers City Commissioners who approved the project and designated space in the city hall park for the erection of the memorial.

The following year on Thomas Edison's birthday, February 11, 1929, the building was dedicated. The news had a great deal of competition. The front page of the *Tropical News* was headlined "Hoover Visits City" because President Hoover was visiting Edison on his birthday. Governor Doyle Carlton had suspended Jerry W. Carter as state hotel commissioner on grounds of incompetence, neglect of duty and misfeasance and Carter refused to vacate the office. County Commissioner W. Stanley Hanson brought word from Tallahassee that the State Road Board would not ignore the need to complete the "missing link of the Tamiami Trail between Fort Myers and Naples" and in Italy, the Vatican represented by Pope Pius XI and King Victor Emmanuel represented by Premier Benito Mussolini had signed a peace treaty healing a breach that had existed since 1870. The abundance of state, national and international news notwithstanding, the *Tropical News* ran a front-page story headlined, "Boy Scouts of Fort Myers Dedicate Goolsby Memorial."

It was quite an occasion. A group of five hundred Scouts, their parents and friends gathered at the site of the memorial. Barron Collier, honorary president of the Royal Palm Boy Scout council and a member of the national council, was scheduled to make the main address but was unable to attend. However, the Reverend O.T. Anderson, the scout chaplain, stepped in and spoke on the value of the Boy Scout program in building character.

The *Tropical News* wrote, "Mrs. Goolsby, dressed in black was on the platform and had a proud smile on her lips as she received from...Kight the Boy Scout emblems won by her son before his death and later assisted in pinning eagle medals on the thirty boys who won the citations."

The architecture of the building was Spanish, built of yellow stucco. "A feature of the council room," ran the account in the *Tropical News*, "is an imposing fireplace at one end, made of rough stone and face brick. It has a wide mantel for the display of Boy Scout trophies and in the center will hang a picture of Thomas Goolsby."

The building stands no longer; it was torn down when what is now the abandoned police station was built. The picture of Thomas Goolsby, according to Mrs. Stewart, is on display in a Scout camp in Charlotte County. Although the building may be a victim of progress, Thomas Goolsby and the values he represented are still remembered and revered by not only Boy Scout Troop No. 1, but by old timers who remember when Fort Myers and Lee County were known as the place "Where Summer Comes to Spend the Winter."

Originally published in "Only Yesterday" in February 1985 in the Fort Myers News-Press.

The Saga of Wild Bill Belvin 1930

William T. Belvin had always been a little different, but still most of the local folks in Lee County were surprised when he came up with so provocative and promising an idea that even the Fort Myers Chamber of Commerce officials were excited. Belvin, forty-eight, had decided he'd live a year a la Robinson Crusoe in the wilds of Pine Island near Burnt Store Road. Ordinarily Belvin would have been written off as a kook, but times were tough.

The year was 1930: the real estate boom had crashed, the country was in the early stages of the Depression and Fort Myers felt its best bet for economic survival lay in positioning itself as a vacation destination. A major obstacle lay in the perception of the rest of the country that Florida was a barbaric wilderness. And Fort Myers was mesmerized, traumatized and scandalized by a local trial involving a schoolteacher and an illegal operation. It was hoped that Belvin's publicity stunt could prevent Fort Myers from being known as the "abortion capital" of the country.

Belvin's self-stated goal was "to force Fort Myers onto the front pages of newspapers by permitting myself to be set adrift nude in the woods for a period of 12 months to prove that Lee County is the finest spot in the United States. To do that, I propose to start out without matches, food or clothing or shelter and maintain myself on the wild plants and animals secured and prepared by methods to which the earth's first men were limited."

Belvin signed a written agreement that was duly witnessed by Ronald Halgrim, secretary of the Fort Myers Chamber of Commerce. And then, one semi-brisk morning in mid-October of 1930, Belvin was taken to the north end

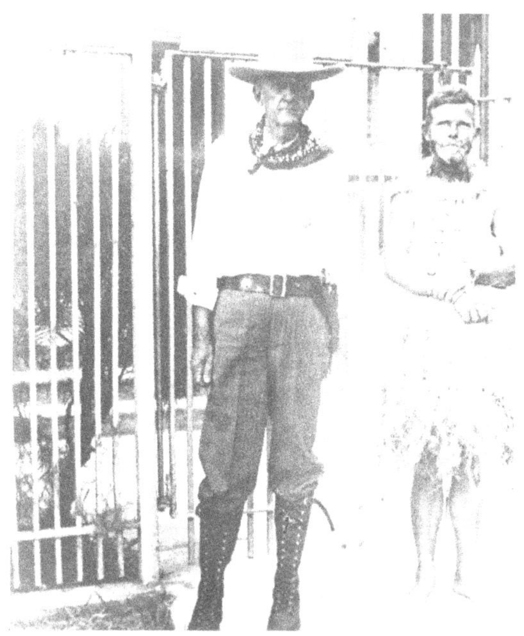

When Wild Bill Belvin (right) returned from a year living off the land in North Fort Myers as a publicity stunt, Sheriff Frank Tippins, himself a colorful figure, arrested Wild Bill for stealing pelican eggs. *Courtesy of Southwest Florida Historical Museum.*

of the new Edison Bridge. He wore a bathing suit, which was to be discarded as soon as he had made clothes from palm fronds. His only accoutrements from the civilized world were his spectacles and an extra pair of false teeth.

Belvin, a farmer, former boilermaker and preacher, planned to build himself a shelter from palmettos in the style of the Seminole Indian chickee. Belvin planned to dine, rather sumptuously by today's standards, on oysters, swamp cabbage (heart of palm to the effete), sea grapes, turtles and small game trapped with hand snares. He also announced his intention to keep a journal of his experiences in ink made from natural dyes on bark.

The year passed and although there might have been occasional sightings of Wild Bill (as he was now known), there was no communication with him. True to his word, Belvin emerged at 3:30 in the afternoon of October 14, 1931. In a front-page story headlined, "Wild Bill Returns to Civilized World Today," the *News-Press* trumpeted his reappearance.

But his timing, due to no fault of Belvin's, could not have been worse. As he returned, the national press was heavily focused on other major stories. In New Jersey, inventor Thomas Edison lay on his deathbed. In Louisiana, Governor Huey Long had ordered the Louisiana Highway Police to guard the governor's mansion while he battled his lieutenant governor to remain governor. Al Capone was on trial for income tax evasion and Belvin himself would face legal problems upon his return.

Halgrim, who had been vacationing at the beach, hurried back to town and organized a reception and banquet, but the most newsworthy reception afforded Belvin was that provided by Sheriff Frank Tippins.

Belvin's first stop as he entered town (wearing a grass shirt and skirt) was at the Royal Palm Pharmacy on First Street (today the site of Sunshine Card and Gifts) where he consumed a soft drink "on the house" as reported by the *News-Press*.

His next stop was at the White Way Barber Shop where he was preparing to divest himself of his beard and shoulder-length hair. However, he had no more than settled into the barber's chair when Tippins arrested him and escorted him bodily to the Lee County Jail.

The charge? Stealing pelican eggs.

Halgrim was dismayed and postponed the festivities. He protested Tippins' action and immediately set about attempting to raise the $500 bail.

For his part, Belvin accepted his incarceration with good grace saying, "Perhaps it is just as well. I understand they haven't much money to feed prisoners with, and I know it would be bad for me to eat too much food at once, which I probably would have done, if I had gone to the banquet tonight." Waxing philosophical, he continued, "Then, too, it will give me an opportunity to study life through prison bars."

It was obvious that Tippins did not consider his prisoner a threat to public safety: the handcuffs were joined only by thin string and the key dangled from the end of the twine.

It was late the next morning before Belvin was released. Halgrim had prevailed upon John N. Thomas, the manager of the Arcade Theatre, to sign the $500 bond. In return, Belvin agreed to speak at four o'clock and nine o'clock to the Arcade audiences. The topic was to be confined to his year in the wilds, not his arrest. However, Belvin voluntarily elected to spend his second night in civilization at the yellow brick jail, which was on the site of today's Justice Center. It was a matter of survival—he was broke and didn't have any decent clothes.

The theatre audiences found his tales riveting and in his talks he revealed his worst foes had been ants, scorpions, snakes and mosquitoes. His year in the wild, he said, "had not been accomplished without suffering." He said his worst experience had been when he cut his foot on oyster shells. "At least four stitches would have been needed under ordinary conditions," he said, adding "but I plastered it with nature's best medicine, raw pine gum, and in a week it was practically healed."

He told of another instance when he considered giving up. High water had driven millions of stinging ants to the high land where he had established camp. And he told of one night when he had awakened to find a rattlesnake sleeping next to him. "But as he didn't snore," Belvin said, "he didn't wake me up. He was just a few feet from me, all curled up when I awoke, but he didn't live long after that. A hefty pine knot did the work."

Belvin also described how he had used his eyeglasses to start fires and he explained he had "deserted civilization a year ago to prove a theory that life could be sustained in the Florida woods without civilized aid." Belvin proved his theory, for the *News-Press* reported he "returned bronzed to perfection and weighing 167 pounds, ten pounds more than when he left."

While Belvin failed to bring national attention to Fort Myers, he did provide a tale that we still delight in sharing today.

Originally published in the November 1991 issue of Lee Living.

A Town's Tragedy: The Illegal Operation 1931

One of the saddest events in Fort Myers's history took place sixty years ago this winter. Seldom if ever written about or discussed, the drama had a distinguished cast of characters, an impact that stunned and divided the entire town, destroyed lives and focused on a topic still controversial and relevant today.

The ill-fated star of this tragic drama was Doris Virginia Long, a thirty-year-old English teacher at Fort Myers High School. The identity of the leading man was never revealed. The villain, at least in the eyes of the law, was Dr. F.K. Armstrong, a local physician.

Miss Long was born in 1901 in New Richmond, Indiana, where her father was mayor at the time of her death. She had come to Lee County in 1925 to teach. A graduate of Butler University in Indianapolis, Indiana, class of 1919, she was, by all accounts, well liked by everyone (students and parents especially) in the then small town of Fort Myers (population 9,082). Never married, she was active in the First Baptist Church and sang both there and at musicals given in the community.

Dr. Armstrong, then sixty-two, had come to Lee County in the early 1900s from New York State where he practiced medicine. He opened an office and a small private hospital in Fort Myers. According to one source, he had a bachelor's degree in medicine and a master's degree in surgery, the only doctor so qualified in southwest Florida at the time. A tall, stately man of liberal and advanced views, he was often in conflict with the local medical community.

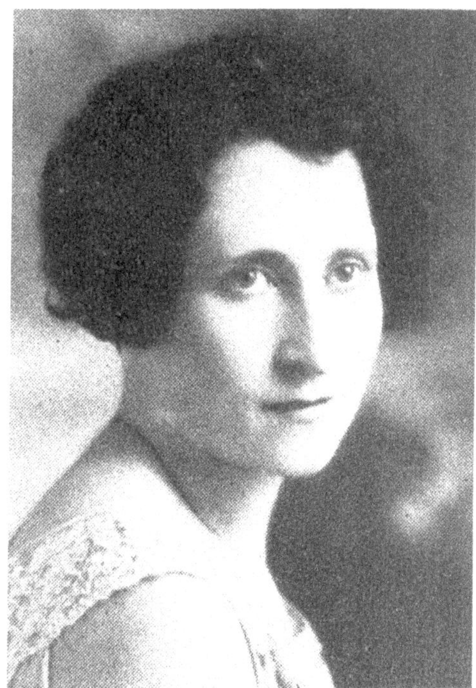

Doris Long, a quiet, soft-spoken young woman, was at the center of one of Fort Myers's most controversial trials. *Courtesy of Southwest Florida Historical Museum.*

The drama began one hot Saturday afternoon in October when Doris Long arrived in Estero on the Collier Bus Lines from Key West, where she'd been teaching since the previous spring. She was ill and at her request, she was met by Dr. Armstrong, her physician and friend. He brought her to Fort Myers and treated her in his clinic where she died the following Monday, October 13, 1930, shortly after 9 p.m. following what the paper would later label an "illegal operation."

The cause of death was initially reported as peritonitis. However, in carefully couched medical jargon, the doctors who testified before the hastily convened grand jury agreed, "the condition which climaxed in Miss Long's death had its inception four or five months ago."

The *Tropical News*, one of the town's two newspapers, reported, "Authorities investigating the case were apparently chiefly interested in determining exactly when Miss Long suffered the injury which the attending physicians attempted to remedy by the operation Monday."

The prevailing sense of decorum was so intense that the operation was never referred to as an abortion, but as an injury. The question that dogged Dr. Armstrong for the rest of his life was whether or not the "injury" was self-inflicted or whether the operation he performed had been an abortion.

If not an abortion, it was then—as he would maintain until he died—an operation attempting to repair the damage caused by a botched abortion performed in Key West.

By Tuesday, the day following Miss Long's death, Sheriff Frank Tippins had received tips from anonymous informants about Miss Long's death and was suspicious for two reasons. The first was that the death had not been reported and local undertaker Lawrence Powell had been instructed not to announce the death until her parents were notified. The second was that although Miss Long had many friends in the area, none had known she was in town.

Later that same day, Justice of the Peace J.B. Conyers, acting as coroner, ordered an inquest and an autopsy. He had empanelled the grand jury, which adjourned after midnight after hearing the testimony of Drs. Armstrong and Winkler and the physicians performing the autopsy: Drs. William Jones and W.H. Grace.

While neither State Attorney Guy Strayhorn nor Conyers would comment, Drs. Winkler and Armstrong spoke openly to the press the next day.

According to Armstrong, once he and the teacher had arrived at his "sanitarium," he had examined her and found "her trouble not immediately remediable owing to her physical condition." He continued, "I kept her resting Sunday and Monday shortly before noon I called in Dr. Winkler to assist with the treatment which had to be discontinued owing to the patient's serious condition."

And then he described one of the saddest moments.

> *After a few hours her condition seemed to improve and about nine o'clock Monday evening the nurse and I who had been in constant attendance of her, left her to take a rest. During our absence she took a large drink of ice water which brought on an intense gaseous condition. She called and the nurse and I hurried to her. Within five minutes she died in my arms.*

While Doris Long's troubles had ended, Armstrong's had just begun and authorities did not move slowly. In the same article that revealed her death and the subsequent inquest, it was reported that authorities were investigating "exactly when Miss Long suffered the injury which the attending physicians attempted to remedy by the operation."

Then the bombshell was dropped.

The results of the autopsy indicated the injury was recent and had occurred within three to five days prior to the death which meant, according to Drs. Jones and Grace, that the abortion could have been performed as late as Saturday, the day of her arrival in Fort Myers.

Armstrong moved quickly as well and retained local attorney E.M. Magaha. Magaha, a former judge, launched an immediate attack focusing on the secretive manner in which the entire investigation was being conducted and his difficulty in getting information. Grand jury members had been legally gagged from speaking about the proceedings as had the witnesses testifying. Results of the autopsy, conducted at midnight at Powell's funeral home, were not made available to the defense attorney. Dr. Armstrong's motion for a second autopsy was denied; however, that obstacle was overcome by permission granted by A.D. Long, the father, who'd sent a hearse from New Richmond to pick up his daughter's body. Once the body was released into the custody of the drivers of the hearse, local authorities were powerless to halt a second examination.

On October 23, 1930, Dr. Armstrong and his office nurse, Josie Hamilton, were arrested and charged with manslaughter. Bond was set at $2,000 for each and they were released immediately.

The stage was thus set for the next act in the tragidrama, the five-day trial that began December 8, 1930. Those five days were laced with black humor and rumors that enraged local doctors and parents of coeds attending Fort Myers High School. Through it all glimmered the memory of the teacher so many people in town had loved, the teacher who'd shared a premonition of her death with a young girl who'd traveled with her on the bus from Key West.

Silent desperation pervaded Fort Myers as Dr. Francis Kennedy Armstrong's manslaughter trial began late in the day on December 8. There was also a sense of community embarrassment that such a thing could happen here. Parents were careful not to discuss the trial and the "illegal operation" within earshot of their children. For weeks, the trial had been very much on everyone's mind, but not their lips.

The sense of desperation, however, related not merely to embarrassment, but also to money. Nationally, the economy was tottering, its downward spiral fueled by Black Friday on Wall Street. Locally, times were tough and getting tougher. Real estate values had plummeted four years earlier and recovery was decades away. Tourism seemed the bright hope of the day, but there was concern that "the trial" would besmirch Fort Myers's reputation and luster as a tourist destination. The wisdom of the majority urged speed. Get the trial over and done with as quickly as possible.

And speed was indeed the essence of the trial's first day. By the time court had adjourned for the day, a jury had been selected and the State had called its first four witnesses. State Attorney Guy M. Strayhorn represented the prosecution assisted by local attorney Watt Lawler who'd been hired by a group of Miss Long's friends determined to see justice done. In addition to Magaha, the defense team included former Judge W.D. Bell from Arcadia and State Senator-Elect Arthur Gomez from Key West.

The jury was composed of six young men. All but two were married. One was a car salesman, one a life insurance salesman, one an officer in a building supply company and the other three either owned citrus groves or farmed.

By the second day of the trial, public interest was so high that not only were the seats in the courtroom filled, but spectators also packed the doorways and even squatted beside the judge's dais. Strayhorn was playing to a packed house as he proceeded to establish that, according to his witnesses, Doris Long had been in good health when she had left Key West on Friday, October10. And jurors were both shocked and literally sickened by the evidence.

Strayhorn had done his homework, for the star medical witness was Dr. William H. Rowlett of Tampa. Rowlett was secretary of the state board of medical examiners and an expert in obstetrics. Rowlett testified "the wound" was "sufficient to cause death" and that death had followed within six to eighteen hours.

But the proceedings were interrupted several times during Rowlett's testimony.

The stricken teacher's womb had been retained and preserved in a jar containing formaldehyde. The purpose was to prove—or disprove—by the size and the nature of the incision that the entry wound into the womb could have been made by an embalming tool. As the womb was displayed, Charles Weiland, the foreman of the jury, fainted and fell to the floor. The doctors, and there were a number present, rushed to his side. He was taken from the courtroom and presiding Judge W.T. Harrison declared a recess.

After lunch, Judge Bell moved for a mistrial claiming that the juror, who was still looking pale, was in no condition to hear the remainder of the case and further, that his impartiality had been tainted because he'd been treated by one of the physicians who'd been a witness for the state. The motion was denied and Dr. Rowlett continued his testimony.

As Dr. Rowlett again referred to the specimen in the jar of formaldehyde, Weiland again became ill. This time, to avoid tainting the jury, Judge Harrison appointed both the defendant, Dr. Armstrong, and Dr. Rowlett to care for him.

While the defense motion for a mistrial failed, another defense motion didn't. Midway through the five-day trial, the defense moved for a directed verdict of acquittal of all charges against Dr. Armstrong's nurse and co-defendant, Josie Hamilton, on the grounds of insufficient evidence. The motion was granted and Mrs. Hamilton was freed, although she remained to testify on Dr. Armstrong's behalf.

In retrospect and judging from the few documents extant today, the medical testimony that formed the core of the charge seems inconclusive. However, people were not as medically and legally knowledgeable as they are today and the state's experts with their important-sounding credentials who traveled from the big city of Tampa must have been impressive. Nonetheless, the defense attorneys also had a couple aces to play.

Over the State's vigorous objections, Adele Baker, a schoolgirl who lived next door to where Doris Long roomed in Key West, was called to the witness stand. The fifteen-year-old girl, one of Miss Long's pupils, testified that they had traveled on the same bus from Key West to Miami and indicated that the teacher had had a premonition of her death.

During that long ride, which required an overnight stay in Miami, Doris Long adjured Adele Baker to "be a good girl" saying, 'You never know what might happen" and telling her that she (Long) might not return from Fort Myers.

A second piece of evidence was a letter in Doris Long's own hand, which she'd written on her deathbed, absolving Dr. Armstrong from all blame in her death. When called as witnesses, both Dr. W.B. Winkler and Mrs. Hamilton confirmed Armstrong's versions of the events that had led to the teacher's death.

Perhaps the one mistake made by the defense was in permitting Dr. Armstrong to take the stand in his own defense. Until this point, he had apparently been quite dignified and controlled. On the witness stand, however, he showed the effect of the strain, creating a furor when he told the packed courtroom that he understood 140 "illegal operations" had been performed on girls attending Fort Myers High School by several local doctors—and he named the doctors. But his countercharges failed to discredit his accusers.

On Friday at 5:40 p.m., Judge Harrison completed his charge to the jury. The jurors retired to deliberate and at 10:20 p.m. that night, returned a guilty verdict with a recommendation of mercy.

According to the account published in the newspaper, "The grizzled 62-year-old defendant received the verdict without flinching. He cocked his head expectantly as the clerk started to read the decision and only a shadow of disappointment passed over his face as he heard the word 'guilty.'"

Defense had four days to file a motion for a new trial and Bell immediately declared his intention to do so. The motion was denied and in January of

1931, Armstrong was sentenced to ten years hard labor at Raiford State Prison. He would not serve any time in prison and the last act in the drama would not be written for several years during which Dr. Armstrong continued practicing medicine in Lee County while appealing his conviction. He won a partial victory in that the Florida Court of Appeals overturned the conviction and the State did not file against him again.

The next scene in the tragidrama was played out nearly six years to the day from the date of his arrest. On the morning of October 26, 1936, Dr. Armstrong died in his private hospital at 1946 Lee Street. Cause of death was the stomach ailment that had led him to move to Fort Myers in 1911 "because it was at the end of the railway line."

Still the drama had not ended. That same evening, without ever knowing of her husband's death, the doctor's widow, Edna Miller Armstrong, died of a stroke at their home at 2225 Henley Place. They'd been married forty-four years.

In his obituary, the *Fort Myers News-Press* wrote the final summation of the man and his medicine. "Fairly well fixed financially," the reporter wrote, "Dr. Armstrong returned to the practice of his profession because he could not resist giving aid to the sick. Starting in those horse and buggy days when he made his calls in a rig hired at L.M. Stroup's downtown livery stable, Dr. Armstrong soon built up a large practice. Many of his services were performed without charge for destitute sufferers."

After a double service at the Engelhardt Funeral Home on McGregor Boulevard, Dr. and Mrs. Armstrong were buried in the Fort Myers Cemetery on Michigan Avenue.

Sixty years may have passed, but Dr. Armstrong is still remembered. And opinions are as divided as when he was alive. Some are convinced he did indeed perform the "illegal operation." Others are equally convinced he was the victim of professional jealousy and his own liberal thinking. The real victim remains Doris Virginia Long, who paid the ultimate price.

Originally published in the November/December 1990 and January/February 1991 editions of Lee Living.

The Town Celebrates its Centennial 1950

Fort Myers had a population ranging between 18,000 and 20,000. The *News-Press* cost five cents daily and ten cents on Sunday. The new Fort Myers High School at Cortez Boulevard had just opened. The year was 1950, the month February, and the occasion was the celebration of the Caloosa Festival commemorating the establishment of Fort Myers in 1850.

That's not to be confused with the centennial currently in the planning stages. The Caloosa Festival marked the founding of the military fort whereas this centennial observes the incorporating of Fort Myers as a town. The Caloosa Festival spanned ten days, coinciding with the Edison Pageant, and was replete with every event a small town could conceive. Some were perhaps unique.

The kick-off was a quiet, even dignified affair, for it was a memorial service honoring Thomas Alva Edison. Held at the new high school's Edison Stadium, nearly two thousand people attended the ceremony. The highlight was a speech given by the economic director for Florida Power & Light, who praised Edison as the "outstanding example of the creativeness and productiveness of a free America."

A special choir composed of 160 voices serenaded the crowd with *I'll Take You Home Again, Kathleen*, Edison's favorite song, along with other songs from the period while seated on a semicircular platform surrounded by palms and white gladiolus.

The days that followed were filled with excitement for those of us fortunate to be here then. The now paved parking lot adjacent to the Elks Club on Hendry Street was an open field. For this event, it became a high-speed racetrack catering not to greyhounds or horses, but to gopher turtles bearing decorations including miniature scenes and landscapes on their backs.

The men around town were suspiciously ill–kempt, grizzled even, because anyone (male, that is) not growing a beard was fined. In fact, a headline in the *News-Press* that week read, "Kangaroos Snatch Up Victims From Crowd and Barber Chairs; Three Whisker Winners Crowned."

Among the hapless victims of southwest Florida's version of frontier justice was Chesley Perry, then general manager of the *News-Press*. Tom Morgan wrote, "Charged with selling advertising, he [Perry] was dressed in a grey skirt, given a sign 'Down With Sears Roebuck,' and ordered to get a wheelbarrow from Sears for the other prisoners." Sears at that time was caddy-cornered from what today is Casa de Guerra Restaurant and adjacent to the Federal Courthouse.

Charlie Knapp of the Gondola Inn (now the site of the new Chart House Restaurant) was convicted in Kangaroo Court for refusing to allow his waitresses to grow whiskers. His punishment, Morgan wrote, "was to deliver a lecture on The Love Life of the Sand Flea." When he responded he knew nothing about the topic, Judge David G. Shapard (a former mayor of Fort Myers, now deceased) said, "You lived on Sanibel," to which Knapp answered, "I only existed there."

Ernest Mitts, who owned and operated the Arcade Cigar Shop, "was accused of running for office, a crime second only to being elected" and two of our city's most distinguished barristers, James A. Franklin Jr. and George Allen, put dignity aside. Of them, Morgan wrote, "James A. Franklin Jr. and George Allen, whose legal objections took up too much time of the court, ate a coconut cream pie held between them while the (kangaroo) cops assisted by pushing their faces into the pastry."

Beauty and bucks were combined to raise money. A contest was held among local high school lovelies to see who could sell the most tickets to the Caloosa Festival events. The contest closed at 6 p.m. four days before the festival began and the results were splashed across the front page in a story along with two column photos of Miss Centennial Martha Freeney and her runner-up, Princess Caloosa Betty Mae Croyle.

The *News-Press* reported that people thronged to buy the books of tickets right up to the 6 p.m. deadline, even forming lines in front of Herman Gluckman's jewelry store on First Street. The ballot boxes were guarded by Fort Myers Police officers. Members of the Business & Women's Professional Club counted the votes, a task which took them until 10:30 that night.

One of the highlights of the festival was the presentation of an historical pageant. The pageant consisted of fourteen scenes depicting important episodes in Fort Myers's history, such as the arrival of Pedro Menendez de

Aviles, the arrival of the first merchants, the first school, the first church and the arrival of the railroad in 1904. While it didn't feature a cast of thousands, the pageant did have a cast of five hundred people, including residents and schoolchildren. More people worked behind scenes sewing costumes, doing makeup and building scenery. Dan Harlacher narrated the pageant, which was done in pantomime. The event itself did not proceed entirely smoothly: a mischievous breeze toppled some of the sets, but it was so much fun that no one really minded.

Babies had their own parade and cowmen groomed their favorite quarter horses and polished their spurs for a procession down First Street. A fiddler's contest was held, a regatta, a fishing tournament, a street dance—and men and women came forward to tell the truth about their ages (some for the first time in their lives) as they competed in the Oldest Pioneer Contest. The Fort Myers High School band played and the glee club sang at and for anything whether it was a gopher race or a fish fry.

That was Fort Myers in 1950. We can't return to being a small town, but we can certainly celebrate what we had and appreciate what we have.

Originally published in "Only Yesterday" in the February 3, 1985 edition of the Fort Myers News-Press.

Dr. Ella Piper Harvey: Thoroughly Modern Ella
1954

Thirty years ago this month, Fort Myers bid farewell to Ella Piper Harvey, a local black businesswoman who died June 13, 1954. Her memory is preserved through her legacy to her people: the Dr. Ella Piper Senior Citizens Center, which stands in a modest concrete block building on the fringe of the Dunbar community.

Harvey, a chiropodist, is respected and remembered by whites and blacks alike for her kindness and the standards by which she lived. Born March 8, 1884, in Brunswick, Georgia, she was the only daughter of Ned Bailor and Sarah Williams. Little is known of her father, but her mother is remembered as having worked for the Harvie E. Heitman family and for initiating the annual Christmas party for underprivileged children in Dunbar, a tradition she began in 1915.

According to research by Vivian Hill, a teacher at Franklin Park Elementary School, Dr. Harvey attended Spelman College in Atlanta and graduated from Professor Rohrer's World Famous Institute of Beauty Culture in New York City. It was apparently at Rohrer's that she studied chiropody.

Hill has Dr. Harvey's diploma, which establishes the date of her graduation as September 25, 1915. For a short time after graduation, she worked as a hairdresser and masseuse at the Twilight Inn in New York. A faded ledger kept in her meticulous script records the prices: a scalp treatment for seventy-five cents, a manicure or pedicure for sixty cents.

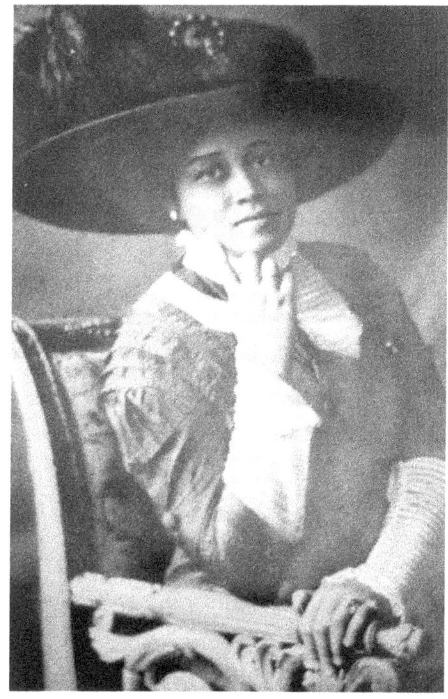

Ella Piper Harvey was one of Fort Myers's most progressive businesswomen. She left an impressive legacy of accomplishments. *Courtesy of Southwest Florida Historical Museum.*

In 1916, she moved to Fort Myers to join her mother, and it was here that she spent the remainder of her life. According to Hill, her first beauty shop was on Jackson Street across from Engelhardt's Mortuary. She was forced to move when the city extended Main Street, taking the land on which her shop was located. She apparently rented that first shop.

In January 1925, she and her husband, Frank S. Piper, purchased land on Evans Avenue from Richard and Julia Barker for $500. It was there that she built her own shop.

Little is known about Frank S. Piper. The groom's record in the marriage license department at the Lee County Courthouse reveals merely that Ella M. Bailor married Frank S. Piper of Washington, D.C., on December 21, 1920, and that the ceremony was performed by Robert H. Pittman, minister. They had no children. No one recalls how they met, only that they were together until he died.

Her mother, Sarah Williams, died in 1926 and her funeral was an event that inspired conversation in Dunbar for years because of the number of people attending and the lavishly beautiful floral arrangements.

Following her mother's death, Harvey took over the Christmas party. She also did something unheard of in those days for a woman of either race: she filed for and received the state's permission to function as a free dealer. The action, which is recorded in the courthouse, enabled her to buy and sell property and to conduct business without her husband's approval or signature.

Hill describes Piper's role in the community by saying, "The coloreds looked up to her as a kind lady. They knew of her, they respected her and they felt very proud, but as far as I understand, they were not closely aligned to her. They did not come to her house for dinner."

Nor did they come to her beauty shop, for her clientele was white and included most of Fort Myers's more prominent ladies. Geraldine Bostelman, widow of Dr. Ernest Bostelman, executor of Dr. Harvey's will, remembers that one of her customers was Mrs. Thomas Edison.

"Ella would go over to Mrs. Edison's to work on her feet," Bostelman recalls. "And every now and then, she'd stop by [and] ask my children, Linda and Ernie, if they'd like to go see Mrs. Edison today. And she'd take them with her."

Bostelman remembers, too, that Harvey was one of the leaders of the Dunbar community, which was then known as Safety Hill. "She was very intelligent," Bostelman said. "And she would give them advice on all kinds of things she felt they should do."

Both Hill and Bostelman recall that Harvey was very active both in her church, the African Methodist Episcopal Church, and in the Daughters of the Elks, Tranquillo Lodge. In the Elks organization, she held national offices. An undated newspaper clipping in the files at the Fort Myers Historical Museum reports, "Mrs. E.M. Piper was re-elected Grand Assistant DT, Ruler of the World at the Elks Convention recently held in Cleveland, Ohio."

In this same clipping, reference is made to her willingness to help young blacks.

> *Mrs. Piper played the part of fairy godmother in preparing a young man, James Johnson, for college last month. She was instrumental in getting the young man a scholarship at Tuskegee for four years and was assured that the folk of the city would aid her in getting the amount of money necessary for him to enter. The promise did not materialize so she gave her personal money and time that the young man might enter on the required date with the necessary requirements.*

Bostelman remembers that Harvey traveled to New York practically every summer and had relatives there. In her final will dated October 27, 1953, her only listed next of kin is a niece, Willie Reed, who lived on West 139th Street.

"She was a friend of Eleanor Roosevelt," Bostelman adds, "and she would stop off two or three days in Washington, D.C., to visit on her way home every summer."

World War II brought a drastic change to Ella Piper's life. For years a widow, she met a handsome soldier, Cleon E. Harvey, a staff sergeant stationed with the army at Buckingham Gunnery School in East Lee County. On March 21, 1944, they were married, according to the marriage license records in the courthouse. Army Chaplain First Lieutenant Willis T. Wrenn performed the ceremony. Harvey was thirty. The bride listed her age as fifty-four, although she was really sixty.

Still another yellowed clipping in the archives of the Fort Myers Historical Museum, apparently from a newspaper in Providence, Rhode Island (Harvey's hometown) reads, "Surprise and consternation seized Providence last week when the mails brought to his many relatives and friends here announcement of...his marriage...to Ella Mertie Piper, D.S.C. of Fort Myers."

The consternation was apparently an omen of things to come. Bostelman recalls, "We asked Ella why she married him. She said, 'He's my security. When I am not able to take care of myself, I will have this young husband to take care of me.'"

It apparently didn't work out that way. Ray Jackson, executive director of the Dr. Ella Piper Senior Center, said he's heard often that the Harveys had been separated for quite awhile before her death.

Her will leaves her husband a bequest of one dollar, and there is a handwritten receipt from Harvey to local attorney George Allen that reads, in part, "This is to acknowledge receipt for $1...thanks very much for your fine cooperation and congeniality during a very trying period."

By the end of the war, Harvey's influence with her people had waned, Bostelman remembers. "It was probably about 1949 or 1950. I don't know what the argument was about, but I remember Dr. Bostelman saying to her, 'Ella, why don't you tell them that's not a smart thing to do.' And she said, 'Dr. Bostelman, they don't listen to me anymore.' But by then, it was after the war and there was an influx of blacks from other parts of the country."

In addition to helping Johnson attend college, Ella Piper Harvey assisted others. Among memorabilia Hill has is a letter dated January 7, 1930, from Cairo, Georgia, in which Minnie Butler thanks Harvey for past help and asks for five dollars to pay her board at school.

Although Harvey had no children of her own, one young woman became very special to her—so close that Hill and Evelyn Sams Canaday thought

Harvey might have legally adopted her, although there are no records of that in Lee County. The girl was Anna Heard, and Bostelman remembers that "Ella said Anna came from a very large family in Virginia. Ella raised her, put her through beauty school, and she worked with Ella in the beauty shop for many years."

Another person prominent in Harvey's life toward the end was C.B. Earle. Bostelman remembers him as a "brother-in-law and retired head redcap from either Grand Central or Penn Station in New York City." Jackson thinks he might have been a baseball player in the Negro Leagues. Among Harvey's effects were a number of uncaptioned photographs of black baseball players.

At any rate Sams and Hill recall that Earle lived with Harvey and Heard in her home at the corner of Evans and Mango. In her will, she provided for them both, stipulating that the contents and the home were to be maintained for the use and occupancy of Earle and Heard, that the beauty shop was to be rented to Heard at a reasonable rent and that, upon their deaths, "all the remaining principal and income shall be paid over to such charities for the benefit of colored residents of Fort Myers as may be selected by my Trustee, Dr. Ernest Bostelman, the then Mayor of Fort Myers and the President of the Lee County Chamber of Commerce."

Although the residence was torn down in the mid-1970s because it would have cost too much to renovate it for public use, the Dr. Ella Piper Senior Center was built directly adjacent to the home site. Today between 1,500 and 1,800 people are helped annually by the center. According to Jackson, they come there for meals and programs that include everything from sing-alongs to lectures on nutrition and crafts.

And watching over them all is the portrait of an elegantly attired black woman wearing a plumed hat. Her kind eyes are watchful, her expression serious. Life was, to Ella Piper Harvey, a serious business.

Originally published in "Only Yesterday" in the June 10, 1984 edition of the Fort Myers News-Press.

George Sanders: Developer of the Edison Mall 1965

The sprawling retail monolith known as the Edison Mall effectively changed the role of the downtown Fort Myers business community forever when it opened twenty-seven years ago this fall. The launching of the Edison Mall marked the movement of the retail center to south Fort Myers from downtown where it had been since the city's incorporation in 1885. And one man, George Sanders, was responsible for its transformation.

Sanders had already built the Boulevard Plaza on McGregor Boulevard in 1959, so he'd had a little experience. "It was real nice and worked fine so I said why don't I try to build one out south?"

That in itself was a decidedly risky, almost revolutionary idea for the times. U.S. 41 (Cleveland Avenue) was two lanes wide. The last building on Cleveland Avenue was the Publix supermarket near Maravilla Street. And, as Sanders remembers, there wasn't another building south of Publix except for a drive-in theater.

Sanders had a bit of a country twang to his slow speech, but his eyes revealed a wry sense of humor and a keenly alert mind as he recalled those days gone by. "At one point," he smiled as he reminisced, "Billy Reynolds [a local realtor and descendant of a pioneer family] said, 'Somebody go get the men with the white coats, because he has lost his mind.'"

But Sanders had confidence in his project. "If you are going to make a dress, you get a pattern. I could take a look at U.S. 41 South and I could see the pattern—I could see what was going to happen."

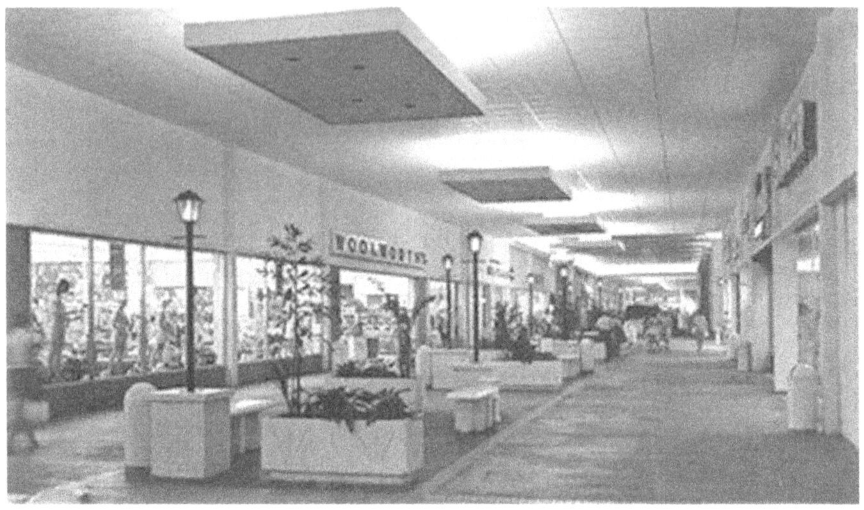

The Edison Mall George Sanders developed was on the cutting edge of shopping mall design and marketing when it opened. Today the Edison Mall, located at the intersection of U.S. 41 and Colonial Boulevard, is referred to in the trade as a lifestyle center. It is currently in the throes of a $10 million renovation. *Photo from author's archives.*

And so the process began. "Mary, my wife, and I traveled to Tampa and Sarasota and looked and looked [at property] and I asked about the price of the land," Sanders says. "It would always be anywhere from $1,500 to $2,500 higher than Fort Myers, and, in some cases, $5,000 higher. We flew to Los Angeles and the prices there were double what Sarasota was. So you felt like you were almost getting the [Fort Myers] land for nothing. I said let's buy it and we did."

One seller had 170 acres on the back end of the strip bounded by Winkler Avenue on the north, Central Avenue on the east, Colonial Boulevard on the south and Cleveland Avenue on the west. The bottom line was that the seller wanted cash—no terms. The cost averaged out to $885.10 per acre.

"I never argued," Sanders said. "I just paid what they asked." And so he acquired the first parcel of what would become the future site of the Edison Mall. Gradually, Sanders acquired the neighboring land on the front until he finally had three hundred acres.

In the meantime, he planted strawberries and the field yielded fruit that local people still talk about. "The land wasn't being used," he said, "so I

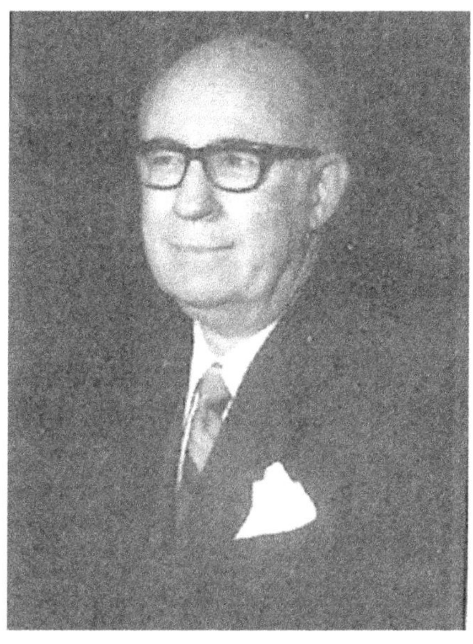

George Sanders. *Photo from author's archives.*

planted twenty acres of strawberries. I have lots of friends who still ask me when I'm going to plant another strawberry field."

On the face of it, planting strawberries might seem like an incongruous act, but not if you understand Sanders's background. In 1942, Sanders lived in Lakeland and worked as a produce broker. He bought cucumbers, tomatoes, peppers and other vegetables and sold and shipped them to northern markets.

Part of the land Sanders was acquiring for the Edison Mall was a huge abandoned orange grove. "The people who owned it had let it go to nothing," he says. "First the rats came to eat the oranges, then the rattlesnakes came to eat the rats. And these snakes were five-and-a-half to six feet long. One day I killed three under one tree."

Sanders persevered and in November of 1965 the Edison Mall opened its doors for the first time. It was anchored by Sears on one end, J.C. Penney on the other and Maas Brothers in the middle along with Lerner's and Woolworth's.

"The response from the community was overwhelming," Sanders remembered and, with understandable pride, shared the fact that he made a bit of retailing history at the Edison Mall. Although it is a common practice now, it was in Fort Myers that Sears and J.C. Penney were housed under the same roof for the first time in any mall anywhere in the country. Sanders recalls this achievement.

"Maas didn't want to open for two years. I said no, you have to open with the rest of them, and they did. Sears had been ready to build where Publix is now. They hadn't quite closed the deal, but they were already figuring to move from downtown. So I sold them the first ten acres and they built their own store and then I joined everything up to them. All the businesses and stores that opened at the mall did fine. I negotiated on a certain volume and they exceeded it. Sears told me that what they would do in [volume] over three or four years, they did in the first year. Maas wanted so much selling [space], so much warehouse, although they had an option to convert the warehouse space into retail. After only one year, they started talking about converting the storage into retail."

Given Lee County's phenomenal growth in the last two decades, it's still difficult to realize just how big a gamble Sanders was taking. He explains, using an analogy: "When I started this thing, it's like I was starting to swim in a pond. I didn't know how far it was to the other shore, it was dark, and I didn't know how deep it was. About halfway through, everybody wanted to help me—some even got out of their boats."

Several years later, he sold the land and built the store for Burdines. "By then," he says, "Fort Myers was really ready [for explosive growth] and they made a complete shopping area unlike anything that had ever been here."

However, by 1979, Sanders was ready to sell. "They [retail businesses] have so many ups and downs, and since I'm a local, they could always find me at mealtimes."

Dealing with the Morgan Guaranty office in New York, he sold the Edison Mall to Aster Properties of Amsterdam. Smiling, he says, "Those folks in Amsterdam, you can't get a hold of them so fast."

Sanders's thoughts about the year 2000? "That's only eight years away so I don't think you're talking about too much change. It [growth] is just going to move south toward Naples and north to Punta Gorda, but I believe it will move toward Naples first. There will just be more and more people."

He won't attempt to predict the pattern today's retail growth will take because "Lee County has changed so much," but he does have opinions about Lee County's future growth.

"We don't want heavy industry [here] and heavy industry doesn't want us, because we can't accommodate them. However, we should be able to attract light industry. Tourists will keep coming in ever-increasing numbers...and the older folks want the sunshine in the winter."

What's in store for George Sanders now? One thing's for sure...no more developing shopping malls. Besides, he describes himself as "perfectly content."

> UPDATE: At this writing in August 2005, the now one million-square-foot Edison Mall is scheduled for a $10 million makeover to begin this month. The enclosed shopping center is to be given a Mediterranean style façade and open-air access to stores opening onto Cleveland Avenue. The Beck Company of Dallas will be the general contractor. George Sanders died in 2002.

Originally published in the Special 2000 Edition, 1992, in Lee Living.

Bibliography

Board, Prudy Taylor, and Esther B. Colcord. *Historic Fort Myers*. Virginia Beach, VA: The Donning Co. Publishers, 1992.

Burke, Walter J. *A Brief Account of the Life of Col. Abraham Charles Myers.* Privately printed, 1976.

Carruth, Gorton. *The Encyclopedia of American Facts and Dates, 10th Edition.* New York: Collins, 1997.

Dahlinger, John Cote. *The Secret Life of Henry Ford.* Indianapolis: Bobbs-Merrill, 1978.

Fritz, Florence. *Bamboo and Sailing Ships: The Story of Thomas Alva Edison and Fort Meyers, Florida.* Fort Myers, FL: Florence Fritz Publishing, 1949.

Grismer, Karl. *The Story of Fort Myers.* St. Petersburg, FL: St. Petersburg Printing, 1949.

Hancock, Almira. *Reminiscences of Winfield Scott Hancock.* New York: Charles L. Webster, 1887.

Hanna, A.J., and Kathryn Hanna. *Lake Okeechobee: Wellspring of the Everglades.* Indianapolis: Bobbs-Merrill, 1948.

Hendry, Captain F.A. *A History of the Early Days in Fort Myers.* Privately printed, 1985.

Johns, Dr. John E. *Florida During The Civil War.* Gainesville: University of Florida Press, 1963.

Tucker, Glenn. *Hancock the Superb.* Dayton, OH: Morningside, 1980.

Warner, Ezra J. *Generals in Blue: Lives of the Union Commanders.* Baton Rouge: Louisiana State University Press, 1959.

———. *Generals in Gray: Lives of the Confederate Commanders.* Baton Rouge: Louisiana State University Press, 1959.

About the Author

Remembering Fort Myers is Prudy Taylor Board's fifteenth published book and is one of her favorites because it is about a very special place: her hometown. The book is a compilation of articles she has written over a span of nearly forty years and will be followed in the fall of 2006 by a companion book, *Remembering Lee County*.

As a freelance journalist, she had more than a thousand articles published in regional and national magazines. She was a staff writer for the *Fort Myers News-Press*, assignment editor and reporter for WINK-TV (CBS) and WBBH-TV (NBC), and managing editor of two regional magazines: *Lee Living* and *Home & Condo*. She is now a freelance writer and project editor with Taylor & Francis, an international publisher of general interest nonfiction and technical and medical books.

Prudy's first book, *Lee County: A Pictorial History*, was published in 1985. Other books include *One Man's Vision: The History of the Port Royal Club in Naples, Florida*; *Pages From The Past*; *Historic Fort Myers, Florida*; *Venice, Florida, Through the Years*; *The Belleview Biltmore Hotel: A Century of Hospitality; The Renaissance Vinoy: St. Petersburg's Crown Jewel*; *Mending Minds, Healing Hearts: The History of the Florida Sheriffs Youth Ranches*; *The History of Barry University*; *The History of Dania Beach, FL: 100 Years of Pioneer Spirit* and *The History of the Dunes Beach and Golf Club*. Her fiction includes *Murder a la Carte*, *Blood Legacy* and *The Vow*.

www.ingramcontent.com/pod-product-compliance
Lightning Source LLC
LaVergne TN
LVHW052342100826
845147LV00021B/1157

* 9 7 8 1 5 9 6 2 9 1 0 1 0 *